The Almost Daily eMOs

The ^Almost Daily eMOs*

*^Mostly Reverent eMails
from
^"Mo." Barbara Cawthorne Crafton

CHURCH
Church Publishing Incorporated, New York

Library of Congress Cataloging-in-Publication Data

Crafton, Barbara Cawthorne.
The almost daily eMos : mostly reverent e-mails from
Mother Barbara Cawthorne Crafton.
p. cm.
ISBN: 0-89869-406-X (pbk.)
1. Meditations. I. Title

BV4801 .C73 2002
242--dc21

2002191185

Church Publishing Incorporated
445 Fifth Avenue
New York, NY 10016

www.churchpublishing.org

54321

This book is lovingly dedicated
to the memory
of
Helen Pond McIntyre
1926–2002

Behold, I tell you a mystery!
We shall not all die, but we shall all be changed,
in a moment, in the twinkling of an eye…

I Corinthians 15:51

Acknowledgments

The people most heartily to be thanked in the preparation of the eMos are the hundreds of people who receive them. It has been a peculiar joy to wake in the morning, creep into my office in the dark and press the "on" button, thinking of the computers blinking to life all over the world, of people reading these little trifles and, perhaps, heading into their days the better for it. Like church, but without the Parochial Report.

Certain individuals have provided a more explicit midwifery: Joan Castagnone of Church Publishing, my wonderful editor, and her colleague, Johnny Ross. S. Robert Hecht used to stab the computer at St. Clement's with a fountain pen and make it work for me; for these and all his other mercies, I am grateful. The Friends of the Geranium Farm on Long Island and the Pickle People of Wellsville, N.Y. and environs have also been most kind. Lastly, to the famous Q—husband, editor, critic and friend—I offer happy thanks.

Foreword

> We can stop at the nursery afterward, I said to Q on our way to what I knew would be the first of several futile visits to the Department of Motor Vehicles (never let your driver's license expire). By the time we left the DMV, my seratonin level was dangerously low. I felt like an Enron perp or the Lindbergh kidnapper. I needed to stop at the nursery for a restorative goodness.

Barbara Crafton gets away with writing like this—writing about everyday details because she is not hokey or sentimental. She sees clearly, with the accuracy of a camera with an expensive lens. She reacts authentically and without guile. She invites us to see and react along with her.

Barbara Crafton engages our minds by holding out to us great discoveries to be found in common details—a virus scan of her computer; the budget of her parish near Times Square; a field set up for a college graduation; two women greeting each other with screams on a train; a CD of "Mrs. Bach, married to Johann Sebastian"—details that lead to ruminations on the shortness and beauty of this life, the joys to be found in unexpected moments, and the tender closeness of those who survived September 11.

As a poet, I sometimes sneak one of my poems into "a talk" I've been asked to give. I would not dare tell the audience that I have done so, lest some shut me out. Inevitably someone who thinks he doesn't like poetry comes up afterwards and says, "I really liked what you said about…" homing in on the poem. Listeners don't need to recognize the formal frame of the poem, the twinkle in their eyes tells me they have connected to it. It has done its job.

Barbara's priesthood infuses this book in much the same way. She does not hide her vocation, but she never sets herself apart either. When we see her as a priest, she is typically going to or coming from a priestly chore, not preaching to us from the pulpit. Her ministry to us as readers is as friend. She is willing to be vulnerable. She knows that we share the same concerns, that we too are enriched by remembering that "Today is the Feast of the Pentecost" or Easter or the Feast of the Ascension.

With an almost childlike innocence, Barbara asks poignant questions: "What did the Unabomber want?" "What does God want you to know?" "Who would want to play malicious tricks on strangers? And why?" She also invites us to try to answer most of them.

I receive well over 200 email messages a day. Even the important ones can be work to read; they tax, they wear down. The almost daily email from Barbara Crafton takes me to another place. A friend has entered my cyber room. She talks to me authentically. I feel I can answer her, and sometimes I do.

Barbara Crafton makes no attempt to help us escape reality: instead she helps us to celebrate it—to live with reality's rough, as well as its smooth, edges.

Louie Crew
November 2002

To The Reader

Conceiving them, initially, as an email version of the daily meditation books which many people use as part of their spiritual practice, I began the eMos as a means by which the members of my parish might have a spiritual essay with which to start their days a few times a week. Thus, the initial group of eMos was called "The Almost-Daily eMo from St. Clement's-in-the-'Hood" a reference to the gritty urban setting in which we lived and worked in those days. It was during the "St. Clement's-in-the-'Hood" period that the World Trade Center was bombed, and some of the eMos from that period provide an on-the-spot look at what it was like to be in New York in those terrible days. Then I developed a serious heart condition, and retired from St. Clement's. As I rested and began to regain my health, the eMos continued, with a new name: now, they were "From the Geranium Farm." The Geranium Farm is not really a farm. It's just our house in New Jersey. It does have a nice garden, though. Lots of geraniums, and lots of other flowers as well.

It might help you to know that the manor house of the Geranium Farm is purple.

I miss the 'hood. 46th Street. Ninth Avenue. I miss St. Clement's. It was a funny, cranky place. It also served the poor better than any church of its size I've ever seen, and more than many churches that are much larger. I was proud to serve there.

Sometimes, you can tell whether an eMo was written in Hell's Kitchen or on the Geranium Farm. Sometimes you can't. Sometimes you can't tell where on earth it came from.

I consider the eMos part of my priestly ministry. Many recipients communicate with me regularly in response to them, sharing their responses and what the eMos have sparked in their own theological reflections. That's what I promised to do when I was ordained: lead people to discover God's presence in their lives and what happens in them.

Why read a book of eMos when you can just get online and receive them that way? Because some of us still like books made of paper and ink. Because not everyone meditates well at a computer terminal. Because many people do their spiritual reading in places other than their offices, and I conceive the eMos as part of a person's spiritual reading in a daily life of prayer. Because many of my readers don't *do* email.

And why are they called eMos? Because many people know me as "Mother Crafton," a more informal abbreviation of which is "Mo." So an "eMo" is an just email essay from me. Enjoy.

Barbara Cawthorne "Mo." Crafton
BCCrafton@aol.com

I

The Almost-Daily eMos from St. Clement's-in-the-'Hood

Asking for Help

"What shall I write my eMo about, Bobby?" I ask. Again. I ask him just about every time I sit down to write one. Sometimes I look into my imagination and find that there is nothing there. So I must ask for help. Sure enough: Bobby leans back in his desk chair, looks at the ceiling, and makes an irreverent suggestion. Irreverent is good. I am off and running.

Asking for help is hard for many of us. All my life, I have wondered what it is that makes it so hard. Being revealed as lacking in something? Having somebody know I'm not perfect? Having to share control of a project? Being slowed down by having to cooperate with someone else? All of the above probably, even though it is true that each time I have asked for help it has made the finished project better.

Interestingly, my reluctance to ask for help seems to be strongest when the work at hand isn't going well. It is as if I fear the widespread discovery of my ineptitude, as if by keeping it to myself I can somehow buy time for it to be magically transformed into a success, as if I might be punished if my work is not perfect. And yet, I don't recall ever having been punished for less-than-perfect work. Odd: I begin to suspect that it is I myself whose wrath I fear.

Such tortured emotions are so far from the spirit of work done to the glory of God! Work done to the glory of God is about the goodness and excellence of the task itself, about sparing no effort to make something wonderful, about enlisting the aid of those whose gifts can make something shine. It's never about lonely perfection or self-absorbed martyrdom. If God did evaluations of the work we do to the divine glory, the first item on the evaluation form would be "Who worked with you on this?"

The Devil and Lee Winston

Lee Winston used to read to the kids in the AfterSchool on Monday afternoons. Sometimes, I would sneak down the back hall to listen: blood-curdling shrieks, frightening diabolical laughs, mean witch voices, and squeaky soprano heroines all emanated from Lee's trained vocal chords, and the kids were spellbound.

One spring weekend afternoon, he went for a hike with a couple of friends and dropped dead at the top of a mountain. The AfterSchool kids were in the funeral: they sat in little chairs, all in a row, and told the people what Lee had meant to them.

For now, I have taken over Lee's story-reading ministry with the kids in the AfterSchool program. It is a way of remembering him that doesn't make me sad—you just can't be all that sad when you're surrounded by thirty or forty kids. So I can think about the day when we stumbled upon the idea of a story ministry here. Or the time when we went over to that great kids' bookstore on Seventh Avenue to buy Caldecott and Newberry Award winners to get started with it. Or how I used to like to sneak down the back hall to eavesdrop on all his different voices, one for each character in the story, and peek at the children, listening so intently. The memories of the good times make us smile. We feel grateful to have had them, even if we have lost them now. Right now, we're working on a book he was reading to them the week before he died. It's called "The People Could Fly," and it is a collection of African American folk tales. They are set in the antebellum South, or in imaginary unspecific times and places. Some feature talking animals. Some are true stories about escaping slavery. The one we read Monday featured the devil and a man named Jack who consistently outwitted him. Mrs. Devil—name of Abbie, by the way—had to keep the fires stoked down there while the devil was up here on earth trying to get Jack.

"Why do they have fire there?" Jenny wanted to know.

"Well, they're in hell," I said.

"Ooooh…" they all said on a rising note, poking each other in the ribs. They know you're not supposed to swear.

"Where is it?" Jenny asks a lot of questions.

"Well, it's not really a place. People just made up things about it, and one of the things they made up was that it is always on fire." In the story, Jack had the devil up a tree. Then he carved a cross in the trunk and the devil couldn't get back down—devil can't get past a cross.

"Why?"

"Well, he's the enemy of the cross. The devil's bad and he hates the cross. So you can stop him with the cross of Jesus." This was getting a little more theological than I had intended.

The devil always scares them. But they laugh every time Jack outwits him. This is what stories do: they give us a model of good triumphing over evil, a narrative in which we overcome those things which we fear may defeat us in real life. In stories, the weak person often triumphs over the strong. In this story, the moral consistently triumphed over the embodiment of evil.

Life is hard. Life can be bitter. Reality is not always a bargain. And in the performing arts—whether it be story, theatre, dance, or just reading aloud—we make reality different, taking it somewhere it may not always go in real life.

It May Be Later Than You Think, But It's Also Better Than It Looks

The trumpet vine in our garden, cut off in its prime in an early spring ice storm, has now been resurrected. It was reduced to a stump, and that's putting it kindly: jagged trunk torn off at the base, splintered vine shafts littering the ground. No potential. But it now stands four feet tall, right on the jagged stump of its demise—who would have thought it? One of its emissaries has traveled twenty feet under solid concrete to sprout a new colony. Another one is intently strangling a peony even as we speak—there is a high degree of recidivism among the trumpet population.

The deficit in St. Clement's budget, at a terrifying $59,000 last month, now stands at $45,000 and will sink to $30,000 or so by next Wednesday. Who would have thought it? Not what one would call out of the woods, but one heck of an improvement.

The parish audit, in tragic arrears since Solomon was a bachelor, is happily nestled, virtuously complete, in the diocesan comptroller's office along with all the other law-abiding parishes' audits. A first for us: law-abiding. Who would have thought it?

Things sometimes look as if they are heading straight off a cliff with no brakes. But life itself has a positive momentum: there are few situations in which some positive intervention cannot produce some positive results. The moral: Don't quit until you've lost for sure. Don't despair until you're sure you've tried everything. Don't have a funeral until you know for sure you're dead. And never underestimate the mighty power of God.

A Visit to America

It was Sanela's parents first visit to America, where their daughter has been living with us and studying at Rutgers for the past four years. After four years of war in Bosnia, during which they saw people shot and houses bombed with people in them, four years during which a famous 15th-century bridge that was the pride of their town was blown to smithereens, four years during which their brilliant daughter was becoming resigned to the fact that she would never get to attend college, becoming convinced that the war had grabbed her future and smothered it like it smothered everything else—they had the chance to send her halfway around the world to live with people they had never met and attend a university they had never seen. In an act of immense courage, this is what they did. She came to live with us. And so their daughter is now ours too, in a way.

And now we all stood in the athletic field, watching the long line of graduates file past the Dean and receive hard evidence of their successful achievement. Sanela was one of fewer than twenty who wrote and successfully defended an honors thesis. Written in a language not her own. Awe is the word best suited to my feelings.

On Sunday they came to St. Clement's, where they hesitantly joined the circle of fellowship, not sure at first if they should, because they are Muslim. They were not accustomed to intimacy in a worship setting. Coffee hour seemed warm and wonderful to them. Then Q took them off on the Grand Tour, the same tour I used to give international seafarers when I was a waterfront chaplain: down Broadway through Times Square, through the Village, pass the World Trade Center, stop at St. Paul's Chapel, take a peek at Trinity Church Wall Street, look right at the tip of Lower Manhattan to see the Statue of Liberty and Ellis

Island, up through the South Street Seaport to see the tall ships and the cobblestone streets, through Chinatown, up First Avenue through the Bowery, past the oldest Jewish cemetery in the New World, through the immigrant neighborhoods of the Lower East Side, past the United Nations, past the world-famous hospitals in the east twenties and again in the east sixties, up Madison past the famous designer shops—Sanela's mother owns a boutique, which in communist days was a state-run store and now struggles through the Bosnian economic transition—over to Amsterdam on Duke Ellington Boulevard to the Cathedral of St. John the Divine, where they went in. They spent over an hour there. In the Holocaust Memorial bay, they found a monument to the dead of Bosnia-Herzegovina. They stood there a long time. They photographed the bronze table to show the folks back home. They were stunned to think that New Yorkers had remembered them in their agony. Vespers was beginning as they left. The organist used the immense trumpet stops at the cathedral's west end. They sound like the trumpet at the last judgment. They had never heard anything so amazing.

Back to Hell's Kitchen, where they were thunderstruck—as we all were—at the Ninth Avenue Food Festival, known locally as the Food Fight. And finally to O'Flaherty's, where we all sat down for a pub meal so my daughter Anna could meet Sanela's parents, even if she had to wait on our table to do so. One of the bartenders took pictures of everyone, and then whole wait staff lined up to meet the Bosnians. A last drive through the neon jungle of Times Square, snapping pictures of horse-drawn carriages against the backdrop of Broadway, and they were ready to call it an evening.

They loved the immensity. They loved the motion. They loved the intimacy of St. Clement's and the awesomeness of the Cathedral. They loved beautiful old St. Paul's. They loved Central Park. They loved it all.

And, showing them this amazing, infuriating, wonderful, terrible place, we loved it, too, all over again. There is nothing to make one appreciate New York like showing it to a stranger.

We are blessed to be here. It is a hard place to be—simple things are hard, like getting to a doctor or buying food. Even taking out the trash is hard here. It's hard to be poor here. But some of the best things in New York are free to all of us, poor or not. So God is still good. Even here.

Still Not Stephen King

There are book signings and there are book signings. The kind you have in a place where the people know and love you is one thing. We've had several here at St. Clement's. Free wine and cheese—they're a blast.

Less satisfying is a book signing in a Barnes & Noble in some distant city where I am not known. I am set up somewhere near the counter next to a table full of my books. People come in and out of the mammoth store, looking for books on car repair or the latest John Grisham. They're usually not looking for warm little books of essays on spiritual topics. You can see them raising their eyebrows at each other—"Who is she?"—and then shrugging their shoulders—"Beats me."

When you arrive in a city on a book tour, the publisher has an escort waiting for you at the airport, holding a sign with your name on it. There is a national organization of these escorts; they meet at the same time the American Association of Booksellers meets. One of them told me that they give an annual award (*in absentia*) to the most annoying author to have toured during the previous year. It's called "The Golden Screw." She said that Martha Stewart has won it more than once. Somehow I was pleased to hear that.

Ninety-eight percent of all books published in the United States do not "earn out" their advance—the upfront payment of royalties an author gets upon signing the contract and commencing the work. You sell books and earn a 10% or 15% royalty on each copy—a dollar or two per book, maybe. It can take a long time to earn out a decent advance at a dollar or two a pop. Those of us whose sales are a little…um…*slow*… are carried by Stephen King. We wish publishers wouldn't give people like Monica Lewinsky million-dollar advances, since celebrity books hardly ever earn out. But they don't ask us.

The only reason they ever take a chance on an unknown author is that the unknown author may be the next Stephen King. Our envious eyes are turned on the madly successful; we struggle not to think of it. We know that we write because we love to write. We know that is enough.

Not everybody is a runaway success at what they do. *Nobody* is one all the time. Everybody likes money, but it isn't everything. Neither is fame. In the end, devotion to our chosen work is what we will take away with us with gratitude for having had the chance to spend our lives doing it.

Anything Worth Doing Is Worth Postponing

I knew I'd be punished for taking Memorial Day off. It really didn't seem that putting some finishing touches on Rosie's two costumes for her performance as Ruth in *Pirates of Penzance* would take that long: some sleeves tightened, a skirt shortened, a neckline narrowed, a piratical-looking vest lined. Nothing to it. I would just get up a little early and knock them right out.

Instead I ran into an old enemy of mine: my chronic inability to estimate with accuracy the amount of time a task will consume. I got up fine—5 a.m. The sleeves were a breeze. The hem was a snap. The neckline was two minutes.

It was lining the vest that hurt. I will not disclose the manner in which I proceeded, as there are seamstresses online as we speak—but it was intended to save me some trouble. I should have known. Once in awhile I believe that I can deviate from the usual way of doing things to good advantage, and once in awhile I can. But ordinarily, all it does is remind me why the usual way is usual.

It was six o clock when I started the vest. I would finish it by seven, haul Rosie out of bed for a fitting and get dressed and run for the train.

At seven o-clock, I was still turning it over and over again, inside out and right side up, again and again, cursing the metallic threads of the vest and the invisible thread I was using to sew with. Cursing my vision—I used to thread a dozen needles for my mother every time I visited her. Now I need somebody to thread mine. I decided I would finish by 8 o'clock instead. I could still get the 9:25 and make it to my 10:00 a.m. spiritual direction appointment only a little late.

At 8 a.m., Rosie left with my promise that the costumes would be delivered to the school by 2 p.m. I was sure to finish by 9 a.m., I thought, although the vest was still putting up a good fight. I would get the 10:07 train. I called my spiritual director to cancel my appointment. I was too frantic and overburdened to go to my own spiritual direction appointment—something wrong with *that* picture.

But the 10:07 train whistle blew and I was still cursing over the damn vest. A little more. A little more. A couple of clumsy tucks taken in the lining that somehow did not fit its partner. Just spiteful.

I finished, hung the two ensembles on their hangers, put a Victorian looking pin at the neckline of the blouse. They looked really nice. I got the 11:07, and was at the church by noon. Better than I deserved.

You shouldn't get yourself into these things, I scolded myself all the way in on the train. Well, part of the way in on the train. Then I thought—*but if you do get yourself into them, all you can do is put your shoulder to the wheel and just do it, no matter how long it takes, and then don't dwell on how mad it made you that you underestimated. Again.*

Long Live the King! No, Not <u>That</u> King.

We were already downstairs for our Mexican dinner that follows the Spanish Mass on Tuesday evenings when a couple I'd never seen before wandered in. Middle-aged, obviously tourists—Irish, from their accents. They seemed a little confused. "We heard there was a picture of Elvis in this church," the husband said.

There really *was* a picture of Elvis here a few years ago. It was a poster from the Episcopal Ad Project: Elvis and Jesus, side by side, with the words "Contrary to popular belief, only one of them actually rose from the dead."

They weren't the first. Visitors from the UK come in every now and then and ask to see the Elvis poster. Apparently a travel writer loved our...well, *spontaneity*, and wrote about us as a church that should be visited. He especially loved the Elvis poster.

This couple was touching. They had a stapled sheaf of photocopies with them. It detailed their Elvis Story: they were big Elvis fans when they were young. In 1961, she became very ill, and he wrote to Elvis and asked him to write her. The King wrote both of them:

Dear Mrs. Colgan:
Just a short note to say I hope you are feeling much better. Take care of yourself and don't worry—everything will be all right.

Sincerely,
Elvis Presley

Dear Maurice—
I sent your wife a get-well message.
Take care of her and yourself.
May God bless you both.

EP

Also included in the packet were a poem Maurice had written about a visit to Graceland, an Irish newspaper article about their decades-long devotion to Elvis, another of Maurice's poems. Their Elvis letters are now in the Music Hall of Fame. Clearly the Elvis letters were the biggest thing that had ever happened to them.

It *was* nice of Elvis to write those notes. He seems to have had a more realistic view of the difference between himself and God than did the Colgans: it was the *divine* blessing he offered the Colgans, not his own. And God did bless them: it was a problem pregnancy that had almost killed Mrs. Colgan in 1961, and today that little baby has made them the grandparents of twin girls.

Celebrities are gods to many people. It is as if they had magical powers, as if their very bodies and their personal effects, items they have touched with their hands, were holy and powerful. I suppose this is even more true these days, when people are so much less willing or able to connect with the real God. There is something poignant about this to me: a movie star or a rock singer cannot save. They are, as the psalmist would say, "a vain hope for deliverance."

We invited the Colgans to stay for dinner. They had just had pizza, they said, and bid us farewell. They left on the same vague, confused note as when they entered, as if they were still searching for something—Elvis, I guess. Or the Holy Grail. But we never have to look that far. The God who loves us is always very near.

Just Act As If It Will All Work Out

A rainstorm appears certain. The show in the theater upstairs—St. Clement's is a theater, you know, as well as a church—has just let out, and the audience is still standing around on the sidewalk, enjoying the stiff breeze, the coolness provided by a darkening sky. How nice, I think—the window boxes for St. Clement's will get a drink.

There are four window boxes. They're in my back garden at home right now. I will drive them in tomorrow and prevail upon Charles to wire them to the iron railing protecting the outside basement stairs. They look lovely already, and the plants are really just getting started. Exciting as a Christmas tree, a window box at the beginning of its life. The dream of its future embroiders its present. Now, the plants stand a bit stiffly upright. They are just getting to know their neighbors in the box. Soon, they will lounge casually against each other and spill luxuriously over the sides.

It may be, of course, that someone will steal them. Or steal a plant from them. This has happened before. I arrived at St. Clement's just after Eric Debigare died of AIDS, and found twelve or thirteen African violets in the little old chapel, gasping for water. I gave them all a nice drink and set them attractively out in the stairwell. By noon they had all walked.

We live and learn.

But I didn't learn not to try just because things don't always work out. I wouldn't want to learn that. Not every wonderful thing you do will work. Someone may come along and ruin it. Somebody may not understand its importance, and may not support you in what's necessary to keep it alive. But that doesn't mean it's not a wonderful thing, or that it was wrong to try. That's what hope is: a vision of a reality into which the current reality *might* grow.

Will we all grow into the full stature of Christ? Will we all live our lives exactly as God wants us to be? I think we will not. But some of us will try. And some of us will come close. And none of us will be denied entry into the domain of realized hope, no matter how far south of its fruition we fall.

On The Seventh Day He Rested, But You Don't Get To

Sunday. Of course, it is the clergy's busiest and most vulnerable day. Busy because—well, do the math. And vulnerable because it's the day when people who don't see you during the week, and don't know what you've been up to, ask you about the things you said you would do. You stand there and struggle to remember what they might mean. If you are lucky, it comes to you and you can converse intelligently. If you're *really* lucky, you've completed whatever it was and can present a nice *fait accompli* with a competent flourish.

But you're not always really lucky. Sunday is also the day when things you forgot you said you would do come back to haunt you, and you scramble to catch up and make whatever it is all right. And it's also the day when people tell you something you're supposed to remember, but you fear you may not because you're old now and you forget everything and anyway you don't have a piece of paper and a pencil on you.

But what a lovely day it is, even so. To see people coming in for worship, to greet them with a smile across the rows of seats. To hear them read Scripture and pray together. To see the children playing on the soft alphabet floor over in the corner. To hear the way the voices resound in the wood-and-glass chapel, a honey of an acoustic space if there ever was one. To see our ethnic diversity become greater every Sunday, and many different people worship side by side, praising the God who made them all and made them all different. To spend even our brief half-hour education period with people who are serious and thoughtful about their faith. To sit in the office now, seeing the street out the open front door, listening to the people walk by, the occasional clip-clop of a horse, the barking of a dog, and catch up on tasks that somehow, today, just can't manage to make me a basket case, no matter how hard they try. To look forward to Evensong, to the voices moving confidently over the ancient chants, led into a contemplative spirit by the sameness of the music and prayer week after week. There are members of St. Clement's whose only worship service is that one, either by preference or because of work schedules. And there is a priest who regards it as a sweet AMEN to a busy day that began many hours ago. The beginning of her own Sabbath time.

We put out the window boxes today. Wired them to the iron railing with picture wire. They'll be gone by the end of the week, somebody says. We now have a pool going—we've guessed how long we think the window boxes will stay in place. I'm in for $10 with my conviction that nobody is going to take them. Not ever. They're going to be with us all summer, until the end of their life span. You'll see. God is always good.

When all was said and done Chris, Rebecca and I guessed that it would last all summer: We won.

Good Intentions and $1.50 Gets You to the Bronx

A trumpet vine update: The place where the wind ripped the trumpet vine apart is now covered with fresh trumpet vine shoots. More than ever before, thick and fresh and lush. I notice, also that the even-more-badly-damaged trumpet vine on the other side of the sidewalk is springing to life too, fresh shoots arising out of the broken branches. And the flowerbed nearby has several volunteer trumpets reporting for duty. By midsummer, Old Trumpet will have taken over again.

Now, there is a way around this. You can buy a product innocuously called RoundUp. You cut a plant in a few places and apply a tiny amount of RoundUp with an eyedropper. The plant dies speedily. RoundUp is something like napalm, I believe.

When Q was a Resident Fellow at Dumbarton Oaks, the beautiful center for the study of landscape design in Washington, D. C., a terrible thing happened. Dumbarton Oaks has a wonderful rose garden—an amazing collection of some of the most beautiful and fragrant roses in the world. Hundreds of them. A new assistant gardener took up duties there, and I guess the guy didn't know what RoundUp was for. When asked to use it in the rose garden, he did—and hundreds of precious roses perished.

I guess that was the end of the guy's career as a gardener. Here is what I derive from this: Good intentions aren't everything. In fact, they're not much. We're responsible for results as well.

I Couldn't Afford To Buy What I've Got

I returned to St. Clement's just before five o'clock and went down to the kitchen to see if I could find Clarence. There he was, surrounded by roasted chickens.

"Darryl was by. He said you gave him a check for $3,000."

"I did?"

'He's coming to get a new one."

"Okay."

I dialed Darryl.

"I'd *like* to give you $3,000. You're worth a lot more than that, of course."

Darryl laughed. "I'll tear it up."

He *is* worth more than that. Everyone here is worth a whole lot. We would never be able to hire people to do what our people do, even if we were rich. It would cost thousands and thousands every week. We don't even have hundreds and hundreds.

Church today was wonderful. Everyone was happy. The singing was great. Even the readings were great, and that's not always the case. People began to clap rhythmically during the closing hymn *Quam dilecta*, which is not a treatment this hymn usually gets. Kind remarks were made about the sermon.

Nothing produces the joy that worshiping God gives us. Lots of things give us pleasure, and some of that pleasure is pretty intense, but there is nothing more lovely than a worshiping community praising God together.

We Were Better Off When We Weren't So Rich

I never had a room of my own when I was little. For the first six years of my life, I roomed with my brothers. When John was about twelve, my mother decided he should have a more grown-up arrangement and moved him downstairs into the den. He came back, though. It was lonely down there. Then, my grandmother and I were roommates. Odd, now, to think that, today, Social Services probably wouldn't have placed me with my own family if I hadn't been born into it—not enough bedrooms.

I thought it was great. There was always somebody around if it was dark and a person got scared. The cat used to come up to the window and one of us would let him in, a co-conspirator.

When, my grandmother came to make her permanent home with us, I thought—a new roommate. A girl, like me. I knew that she would love my doll collection and the actual stuffed pheasant and the books and toys that filled most of the room. My grandmother was so gracious that it only recently occurred to me that she might very well have preferred not to share a room with an 8-year-old.

I think of her today. It is hot today, and we are not air-conditioned here, as we were not in my childhood home. Nobody was in those days. Sometimes I would complain of the heat. In response my grandmother would tell me stories of how cold it got in Minnesota, where we were from. How you could pour out a pan of water and see the frozen droplets fall to the ground. How a soap bubble would freeze in the air and you could play with it. How one of our cats went wandering and came back without ears or a tail—frozen off.

That's my first memory of knowing how powerful words are. Words have power. I would begin to feel grateful for the heat. I would begin to think about keeping warm. I would pull a sheet up over my shoulders, moments after I had thrown it desperately off my entire body. And we would subside into sleep together, my grandmother and me, comfortable and cool no matter what the thermometer had to say about the matter.

What the Garden Shows

Monet's garden at Giverny is as lovely as the many paintings he did of it: the Japanese bridge, the lily ponds, the blue, blue irises. We saw a plant we think Monet may have invented himself, just for its Impressionism: its flowers float in layers, points of white. But we also saw gorgeous roses grown into trees, an island of bamboo that almost made us think charitably of our own rampant bamboo patch, pots and boxes of red geraniums spilling out of every window and over every fence, banks of fragrant lavender lining the walkways. It was a pleasant jolt to see plants we have in our own garden in this masterpiece, and we felt vaguely proud, as if we were participants in that genius.

And so we are. Not in Monet's genius—God gave that to him alone—but we participate in God's amazing creative force. When we create, or cooperate with God's creating, we are one with God in that moment. It is us at our very best. Our creating is God at work in us.

My garden is my highest achievement, said the old painter after thirty years of work on his beautiful retreat. It is a painting, in a way: carefully put together to create a natural, accidental effect in a technique that is anything but accidental. Everything is planned, and nothing looks it.

There's a reason for everything, people say. In the Impressionism of human history, certain dots of paint don't appeal to us much on their own. It is in the canvas that they take their proper place, contributing to the beauty of the whole, if only by providing a dark contrast with the bright, a sadness to allow us to know what happy is.

On July 7, just after finishing up the hymn "Faith of our Fathers," whose last line is "We will be true to Thee 'til death," I collapsed on the chapel stairs. Then I went to the hospital and had an angioplasty. I headed back to work— too quickly— I think, for I didn't seem to be getting much better. The eMos got a little spotty, as did a lot of other things. I didn't realize that everything had changed in an instant, and was to keep changing all fall—we were, after all, heading innocently into September 2001.

Fear of Praying

"I'll pray for you," we always say when we hear of someone who is ill or in trouble. But some of our friends don't say that. They say things like "I'll keep you in my thoughts" or "I'll be thinking of you."

Why might somebody be reluctant to own up to praying? I think it's a fear of looking foolish. Prayer is going all out, opening your future and the future of the one for whom you pray completely to God, showing the complete underbelly of your powerlessness and asking a power beyond you to enter into the situation. Boy, I'll feel dumb when nothing happens. And so they don't pray. They don't go out on that limb. They don't hope.

But prayer is brave. It's willing to look foolish, to put all its eggs in one basket. To push forward, even if you don't know what's going to happen. I long so for this healing, I will stand up and say so, because I will do anything—anything—if there's even a chance that it will make it happen.

Of course, prayer doesn't make things happen. Prayer allows us to be a part of the mighty stream of God's love that already flows through and around the one for whom we pray. We do not introduce that person to God: God knows that person very well already.

My father and mother called me one night, rather late in the evening for them. They had been to a healing service, they said—this, too, was most unusual. Our family didn't go to things like that. After the service was over, they were filled with an inner peace quite unlike anything they had ever experienced before. They just drove around a little before going home, allowing the experience to sink in.

"I don't know what's going to happen," my mother said. "But I know I have been healed."

This was a year or two before she died. Her last years were a checkerboard of hospitalizations and setbacks, until the final one that took her home. She did not recover her physical health. But she had reached and claimed a healing. She had been willing to appear foolish. Prayer is brave like that.

The Great American Game

"I'll take your two tickets if you don't want to go to the ball game," says Geri. "I've got a waiting list."

Geri is planning a parish trip to see the Staten Island Yankees play the Brooklyn Cyclones. There are only 25 tickets, all of which were snapped up immediately. I got two of them. But that was before I became ill, and now I'm not sure a three-hour game in the sun is a very good idea.

Russell—being from the UK—is unfamiliar with baseball. Cricket is his game. "There doesn't seem to be much actual movement in baseball," he says carefully. Russell is a most polite visitor to our shores. Everybody laughs at that observation. Certainly, it is the gospel truth. Just about every player stands still as a stone for the entire game. Once in a while the pitcher communicates with the catcher by scratching his nose or grabbing his crotch—the baseball diamond is the setting in which a man can do this and it's normal—and once in a while the batter hits the ball and there is a tiny flutter of movement in the direction of the hit. But, for the most part, nobody moves. The back-and-forth competitive thrill of soccer or rugby or cricket just doesn't happen in baseball.

"Baseball and Thanksgiving are the two things you have to understand if you want to understand Americans," my friend Doug says. I tell Russell that. He won't be here for Thanksgiving, when we all behave for a day as if we were descended from the people of the Massachusetts Bay Colony, whether our surname is Leibowitz or Andersen. People surnamed White Deer or Least Heat Moon don't have this compulsion, their inherited memory of the first Thanksgiving being rather different. Russell will have to make do with baseball, the Great American Game, an inexplicable game choreographed like a 17th-century dance.

I must remember to tell him about the Negro League and about Jackie Robinson and how mixed a history baseball really has in the United States. Maybe he can watch the dreamy 734-episode documentary on the subject by Ken Burns. Maybe he can watch *Field of Dreams*.

Or maybe what he needs is just to go out and hit a few. Then he'll get it.

Give It Up

Don't eat salt. Got it.

No cholesterol. I'm there.

No more than 20 grams of fat a day. Okay. I'm working on it.

Drink lots of water and no caffeine. I'm righteous on this one.

Reduce stress. Big problem.

Adhering to a firm schedule of work-time and off-time helps. For the first time since infancy, I am getting enough sleep every night. I only toss and turn on the nights when I fall into what is emerging as an extraordinary reservoir of ancient worries, resentments and hurts, a deep reservoir I didn't even know was there until I slowed down and had time to think. Things that happened months or even years ago creep into my conscious memory and burst into flame there, and I literally tremble with anger. Or choke with tears. Or catch my breath in fear.

All of these things were things I thought I had, as we say, *worked through.* And, to a large extent, I had. But the scars of our lives continue, and sometimes they need to be stitched up again, even if you've already stitched them up once. Or twice. Or more.

People sometimes approach me in confession with old resentments they thought they had let go. "I don't know why I'm thinking about this now," they say, "I haven't thought of it in years. I don't know what's wrong with me." Well, what's wrong with *me* when *I* do that is what's wrong with everyone else: we're sensitive to emotional triggers. We have weak places that remain shaky no matter how confident we become. And, when we find ourselves in a weak place—ill, suddenly unemployed, alone—all of the ways in which we have ever been in pain come crowding back upon us.

And what to do? What you do is what you did when it happened the first time: take it to God in the way you take things to God. Make a sacramental confession, if it is your way to do so. Go to a healing service. Enter God's presence through centering prayer. Seek out a spiritual director. Avail yourself of psychotherapy—again, or for the first time. Talk to someone you trust, and listen to what that person tells you in love. Some or all of these things are the way out of the woods for you. You do not have to stay angry. Or hurt. Or afraid. These things are not God's will for you. Not ever.

It is a great gift for me to have found my hidden reservoir of pain. It reminds me of something I must never forget: our need to call upon God is continual. Not much on earth is ever settled; that is part of the human condition. And nothing is beyond the healing touch of God; that is the divine condition.

The Golden Years

"Well, we didn't run out of food right on the spot," Russell says. That's good. Seth had told me we were running low, and that our new grant from the Feds doesn't start until the end of the month. Yesterday was little lighter than some days—beginning of the month, you know, and people just got their checks. So that helped. But we still had 329 people. It wasn't all that long ago that we were averaging 150 people a week. When they say on the news that the economy's in trouble, I'm a believer. We had 329 reliable indicators today.

So many of them are elderly—half of them, or even more. My mother did not live to be elderly: she died in middle age. She had everything a person could want except good health. She never faced living alone on a tiny income in one of the most expensive cities in the world. She never had to know what it was like to struggle out of bed and cram swollen feet into old shoes so she could hobble out with a rickety shopping cart and line up in front of a church for food. She had no firsthand knowledge of malnutrition, save that which her illness would impose upon her as her life drew to its close.

I have always wished she had lived longer. But I would never have wanted her to endure such things—old age ought to be a time dignity and reward, but it is so often anything but that. To be part of a church that enters with compassion into the lives of people who carry such heavy burdens is a great honor. When we serve the poor, Jesus told us—more than once—we are serving him. When you bring an extra can or two of food for the offering basket on Sundays, you are feeding Christ himself. When you tell a friend about your work at the food pantry and encourage him to do the same, you are spreading the gospel in an important and utterly concrete way.

St. Clement's will always be able to meet any challenge if we offer ourselves to God for service in complete humility. And humility ought to be easy for us—we don't have much in the way of riches to get in our way.

The Ghost of St. Clement's

"Did you light the altar candles?" Bobby wants to know. It is 93 degrees Fahrenheit outside, maybe a breezy 91 degrees in my office. I ain't lightin' nothin'.

"No, I didn't," I say.

"Well, I was just up there and they were lit."

This is strange. It is Monday and there's no Eucharist on Mondays. Morning Prayer has been over for hours.

"No wonder they burn down so fast. I've gone up there in the middle of the day a few times and found the AIDS candle lit."

"It's a miracle, Bobby," I tell him.

"Whatever."

Maybe there's a ghost in St. Clement's. A dead priest, maybe, who says Mass in the middle of the day for other ghosts. I am scribbling notes for a book about St. Clement's—fiction—and it's not going very well. I am not a fiction writer. Maybe that's because truth is stranger. My book about St. Clement's—called St. Aidan's in the book, because there isn't a St. Aidan's in New York—is stilted and posturing. Thus far, it is quite boring. Perhaps I should put the ghost in to liven things up.

Of course the candles are for a Mass. *Of course* all the other ghosts go. Everybody goes to every Eucharist, the living and the dead, those who were faithful in life and those who were faithless. We all go, even when we stay home and sleep the morning away. The Body of Christ assembled prays and celebrates in the midst of the communion of saints—"Joining our voices with angels and archangels, who forever sing this hymn to proclaim the glory of your Name."

Hot As Hell

Boy, is it hot.

It's fun to talk about how hot it is. Who doesn't like to complain with a friend? A rare spirit of fellowship takes hold of many—well, *some*—New Yorkers at times like this: even strangers pass one another in the street, make eye contact and then they both shake their heads in resignation, an unspoken "Boy, it's hot" hanging in the air between them. The cats find places where they can lie flat; cats know that if you can get flat, you can get cool, even if you're covered with fur.

The kids pretty much live under the sprinklers at May Matthews Park across the street. They come in drenched, and evaporate within minutes. We're having the Spanish services down in the parish hall this evening—not as beautiful as the chapel, but a heck of a lot cooler, and it has been proposed to me that we do the same for the healing service tomorrow night. We'll see.

This is good practice for hell. I think. Just in case. Basically, though, I don't believe in it. I think we raise enough while we're here to suffice. God is good, and does not, as we say, "desire the death of a sinner." I believe that God continues to care for us, and to govern our being, after this life is finished. Those who need to put certain people they don't like in a bad place for eternity should, perhaps, consider a God other than the one who became incarnate and died for our sins.

Out of Touch But Not Out of Mind

Hey.

Long time no see.

The mouse is broken on the only computer in the office that can do email. Well, not the mouse exactly, but the port into which the mouse sticks its rotten little—no, I won't attack it personally. Suffice it to say that I haven't been able to email for over a week. Terrified as I was of the download, I finally logged on with the keypad—you know, *keypad*, before there was such a thing as the mouse?—courtesy of Bobby Hecht's antique computer skills.

What did we do before we had email? We avoided each other by means of our answering machines. What did we do before we had answering machines? We sat and listened to the phone ring and ring and later said we hadn't been home all day and that we were very sorry. But we weren't sorry. We were glad—or we ought to have been. But, in those, days, we didn't know yet what a mixed blessing constant communication could be.

There are plenty of messages we'd just as soon not receive. Ease of communication does many good things for us, but it also loads additional obligations on us without asking us in advance. There is such a thing as being too connected.

Still, I have missed the eMos. Missed writing them. Missed making Bobby give me topics. "Write one about how you had trouble sending email," he said today, and I was off and running.

Writing a story when you know your audience is fun. It is no shot in the dark, like writing something and sending it off to a publisher you've never met. Actors know what it is to come to know an audience, something they must do at every performance, since every audience is different. The delivery that killed them Friday night leaves them smiling politely on Saturday afternoon, and you are left to figure out why, and how you can win them back. Do it for long enough, and you know lots of ways. Do it for long enough, and one of them will work.

Less Than a Month From Now, I Would Wonder How I Knew to Write About Dust

There is too much dust in my office. Of course, there is too much dust everywhere in New York—you'd think we were in Santa Fe. Too many old buildings, old plaster, old furnaces. But the dust in my office provides a record of something I'd just as soon we skipped: the layers of mistakes, missed deadlines and undone tasks.

Here is a package of fountain pen cartridges. I have had several lovely fountain pens in my life: I bought one to celebrate the publication of my second book, another one just because I liked its looks. I have an augustly fat dark red Mont Blanc—its gold nib is split, though, so it's waiting to go to pen rehab. It's been waiting for about five years. I vastly prefer writing with a fountain pen to writing with any other instrument, and I prefer writing in a notebook and crossing things out to composing on a computer. Even so, all my lovely pens are either out of commission or lost, having suffered the fate of most small objects that find their unfortunate way into my possession.

The pen cartridges have been sitting there for at least nine months, ever since my nice dark blue Waterman went missing. I should move them. Or I should get another pen so I can use them. Or I should get the Mont Blanc fixed—no, it doesn't use cartridges, so that wouldn't help. I could give them to someone who also uses a fountain pen. At the very least, I could dust them. They shouldn't be allowed to sit here so forlornly, covered with dust, mute reminders of my many failings.

Dust, I suppose, is tiny particles of the earth, all of it: of trees and people and meteors that crashed here millennia ago, of dogs' fur, crushed butterfly wings, pulverized diamonds. Dust is the final earthly appearance of everything—*You are dust,* we say on Ash Wednesday, *and to dust you will return.* Isn't *that* the truth? All of the things you didn't finish and all the ones you did, all alike will be dust someday. Only God remains, and only that part of us that bears God's image endures.

It Takes Hell's Kitchen

"Your mama just called, Maria," I say. "Did you know that?"

Maria rolls her eyes. She is thirteen, as of a few days ago. She has been coming to St. Clement's since she was six. She and her mother come to the Spanish-language Eucharist on Tuesday nights and to the dinner afterwards. Sometimes her dad comes, too, if he has the evening off.

What a pleasure it is to watch the AfterSchool children grow. Having been here, now, for more than five years, I remember all of them at earlier stages in their lives. I remember when Sean, who is autistic, was unable to answer a question. Some of his answers are still quite unusual, but he's interacting, and that's a miracle. I remember Erika, who spent her years from ages 5 to 8 with us. She used to come and see me in my office sometimes, when she was feeling sad. She would move around the room from object to object—"What's this? What's this?" I saw her on the street the other day, taller and more mature but still definitely Erika. "Do you remember me?" she wanted to know. Oh, yes, I certainly do.

Few things are as satisfying as knowing that the kids feel safe and cared-for here. It is a great honor to be someone to whom kids can turn. It is an especially great honor when it continues through the teenage years, a time of difficulty and no little danger. I remember feeling closer to adults other than my parents when I was young, and I remember very well that there were things I craved that I could only get from them. It really does take a village to raise a child. St. Clement's makes a pretty good village.

The Only Good Meeting Is a Dead Meeting

In the past two weeks, three—or possibly even four—meetings have collapsed before drawing their first breath. The meeting may be on at 9 a.m., but it's off by 4 p.m. People just can't make it. Away, on vacation or somewhere. Something about the last two weeks of August does that to us: we just can't make it. We're going to have to reschedule.

You call people at the diocesan offices. They're all away, too. Call anywhere, sacred or secular—you get a faintly triumphant voicemail recording: "I will be out of the office until Wednesday, September 4th."

This is not the end of the world. I believe that human society is improved whenever a meeting is canceled anywhere on earth—we feel the benefit right here when somebody in Jakarta or Manchester has to reschedule with a colleague, the slightest lightening of the burden of the world's work. There will be plenty of time to drive ourselves crazy with meetings a little later on. Anything that can't be settled before then will just have to wait.

The longing to rest and refresh is a gift from God. It is intended to lead us in the direction of self-care, a direction in which some of us are strangely unwilling to go. We are afraid of appearing lazy. Some of us are even irrationally afraid we *are* lazy, however impressive our mountain of accomplishments in life. *But what have you done lately?* A cruel voice within us asks snidely, and it turns out that "lately" means "within the last ten seconds."

Oh, lighten up. If something is important others beside me will see it and it will happen. If they don't, perhaps it is not as vital as it appears to me. Put your feet up and have a lemonade.

I Only Have Eyes For You

"Let me tell you something, the ophthalmologist says as he finishes my eye exam. "Your glasses are too big. People haven't worn these since the eighties."

"Yeah, my daughter has been scolding me about them for a few years now. I was sort of waiting until they wore out."

"Well, that's stupid. Glasses don't wear out." He is the son of an Italian longshoreman. I like going to him because of the abuse he heaps on me. It reminds me of my happy years on the waterfront.

With the help of his assistant, I have soon picked a pair of chic, smaller glasses that, I feel certain, will satisfy even Anna, the fashion god. They'll be ready in a week.

"Besides, these are way too weak. These are from several years ago. What did you do with the ones I gave you last year?"

"They were hurting my ears."

"And you couldn't take ten minutes to come back and let me straighten the temples for you. Boy, is that dumb." I really love this guy.

I have seen the world through a frame since I was twelve. I remember walking into school for the first time in my new glasses, thinking that I looked more than usually studious. I don't recall being distressed by having to wear them, or wondering if men would make passes at me—I probably hadn't encountered Dorothy Parker at that stage. I feel naked without them, and I look a little naked, too, kind of rabbit-like, I like glasses because the frames hide the shadows under my eyes, halfway conceal the evidence if I have cried recently. Without them, I am clumsy, disoriented, unlike myself.

"Now we see through a glass, darkly," Paul said about the spiritual life while we are here on the earth. He must have had a poor prescription;

I see better through a glass. I think that my glasses are like a spiritual lens that I might think of putting on, a decision to focus on the goodness of God and allow the rest of the world to be its backdrop, as clear or as cloudy as it needs to be in order for me to see what I need to see: God.

My natural eyes don't see well enough. I need help to see better. Natural and unassisted is not always the best thing; lots of times people just need help, and they shouldn't feel ashamed about asking for it. But a lot of us do. My recent illness is teaching me a painful lesson about how far down the road I had gone toward thinking that I was my own God, solely responsible for getting everything done that needed doing, unwilling to let anything slip out of my anxious grasp.

Ah, but I am not God. I need glasses to see. I need a lot of things I do not possess on my own.

Your Weakness Can Be your Greatest Strength

"So what should I write my eMo about?"

Bobby sits up in his chair and thinks a minute. "Write it about losing Russell."

That's a good idea. St. Clement's folk first "met" Russell through an eMo, one that wondered what on earth he would think of us once he got here. And now he has spent two months with us, and will fly home on Thursday. So what *did* he think of us? You'll have to ask him. But I think that a number of people were surprised at how quickly he became a part of us, and by how quickly we felt part of him.

Most parishes are not close enough to a theological seminary to have seminarian assistants on a regular basis. It's an honor to have a part in the training of so many priests. It's nice to think they'll be telling congregations in Des Moines—and now, Cambridge—about something odd that happened here. So many odd things happen here: they'll never run out of stories.

I think it's important for people in training to have a chance to work close to the ground. In places where money is more plentiful, there's not a lot for a seminarian to do: they have large clergy staffs, so there aren't many chances for a student to preach. Clergy leadership and planning processes are well insulated by plentiful support staff, so there are not many ways in which a student can become part of actually planning and bringing off a parish event or service.

Look at them properly and our weaknesses provide opportunity for developing greater strengths. Who wouldn't want more money—lots more, and fast—or a larger clergy staff. I sure would. But it is also true that not having these things forces us to work together and makes us take pleasure and pride in things that, in other places, might not be worth mentioning. It prods us toward ways of solving problems that would not occur to folks who have a lot of money to throw at them.

What is true for St. Clement's is also true for you. Every unhappy thing in your life gives you an opportunity to become stronger than you were before it hit. Every misunderstanding gives you a chance to learn something about reconciliation, or at least to value in a different way the love you have lost. That doesn't make bad things good, but it does give us all a way to redeem our sorrows and find joy where we thought there was none.

I bet Russell will be glad to be in his own room again. I bet he'll be glad to get a cup of tea that didn't start its life as a tea bag and a cup of tepid water. He'll be glad to study again. And to see his friends and colleagues. I'll bet he'll be glad to start out his ministry in a richer church than St. Clement's, which won't be hard. But I hope he has seen enough here to know, in a new way, that human limitations—as final as they often seem to us—are not limitations to God.

September 12

Hell's Kitchen is a strange place today. You could cross against the lights on Ninth Avenue at mid-day and not even look both ways. Anna and I walked out for breakfast and couldn't find a newspaper—completely sold out. We went into one of those junky souvenir shops and bought a few postcards of the New York City skyline the way it was until yesterday: the twin towers at night with a pearly moon in between them, the twin towers by day with a harbor full of sailing ships, the city viewed from up here with the twin towers dwarfing everything else.

Last evening's prayer service was beautiful. The rabbi from the Actors' Temple and several of his congregants were there; he gave us a blessing in the ancient tongue of our common faith. People stayed for dinner afterward—sooner or later, everything at St. Clement's turns to food.

And, after dinner, we began to share our thoughts about the ways of God. Many were in tears, asking the old question that has no answer: Why? Why? How can God be good? What does it means that God is love? Where does this evil come from, then?

When the people of God gather to mourn and to wrestle together with painful questions, the Holy Spirit is deeply present. We don't get neat answers when we do this, but we get what God promises—which, by the way, has never been answers. God promises to be with us—"always, even to the end of the world," as Jesus puts it.

Some of the people kept vigil all night, unwilling to leave the sanctuary and the comfort it contained. Here they stayed, as others came and went around them. Today, a steady stream of neighbors has brought first aid supplies, food, men's socks and underwear, money for the children of slain firefighters and police officers. People call from other cities—

visitors we have had, those who came for a New York weekend and found themselves helping in our food pantry, former seminarians, other clergy. It is hard to focus on normal work.

Just now, the wind has changed, bringing with it the acrid smell of smoke from Lower Manhattan. I see a light haze outside. There is a light haze across the nation. There is a light haze around the world. When a child of God is injured, we are all injured. When a child of God is overtaken by a spirit of hate, we are all in danger of infection. I cannot help breathing in the smoke, but I can guard against the infection of hate. In the days to come, those who follow Christ must exercise special care to be part of the solution and not part of the problem. Already bias crimes against Americans of Arab descent have been reported in our city. Let us examine ourselves and guard our tongues, even in the midst of sorrow and anger at this terrible crime.

Blessings on you. Please know that I am praying for you, and please pray for the city we love and the brave sons and daughters it has lost.

Ordinary Life Is Our Best Weapon

It is hard to focus, I find. Everything I had planned to do seems trivial now, and I can't do some large efficient thing to make the World Trade Center come all together again. The collapse of the towers, viewed so many times on so many televisions, seemed ridiculously slow and surreally genteel: down they went, like stacks of cards, in a process so uncanny it feels like it would be no impossible task simply to reverse the film and see them come up again. And yet, it was anything but genteel. We were looking at chaos, and we couldn't believe our eyes. We don't know what chaos looks like, or how to see it. We keep thinking it's a movie.

The people who wrote the Bible understood it better. They were at the mercy of more things than we are. More illnesses were fatal, more accidents final defeats, more wars indiscriminate slaughter. We, on the other hand, have become used to calling the shots. The idea that there might be a situation in which we are powerless is a new one for us. It's not in our script. And now we begin to suspect that this is not a movie.

The people who wrote the Bible always called upon God bring order out of chaos. Defeated by many things that no longer defeat us, they knew of their need with more accuracy than we know of ours. It is easier for us to try to be God—but it never works. It is easy to believe ourselves to be in charge. But we are not.

Many of us have spoken of God's power and goodness this week—more than a few by wondering what happened to it. Each time we discover anew that life is hard, we wonder about that. But our holy Scriptures were written down by people who also knew that life is hard, and knew it better than we do.

They knew chaos so much more intimately than we do—and yet, somehow, they found a way to keep going with the tasks of life. They didn't stop grinding flour or weaving cloth or building pyramids or discovering mathematical formulas. They kept on, even when the tasks of ordinary life must also have seemed trivial.

And we can focus on our tasks, too. We've got a big food delivery tomorrow, and nobody else is going to unpack it for us. We've still got to do the church bulletins. I still must write a fundraising letter, and the one I already wrote now seems utterly wrong. So rewrite. Pack those bags. Do that report. Run that errand. Improbably, the most efficient destroyer of chaos is not a mighty army, but an ordinary life, well lived. Have one. May your day be a day more like other days than any day you've had this difficult week.

It's Tough All Over

How're ya doin'?

People are asking each other that question with more than the usual reflexive cheer we usually employ. They exchange the slightest of significant glances, and each knows what the other means: How are you really doing? Did you lose anybody? Are you in distress? Can I help? Then one will say something like "This is a hell of a thing, isn't it?" and the other will answer with a slow shake of the head.

I heard some fool on the radio this morning telling a reporter that he wants to punish "the Arabics," that he doesn't want them in New York. I've been wondering ever since whether his mean-spiritedness was exceeded by his ignorance or vice versa, and I just can't decide. Help me out.

We went out to the two bodegas nearest us: one is owned by a Yemeni family and the other by a Lebanese family. We asked them how they were doing. They were okay, they said. Just to be sure, I told them that they should come and get us if anyone gave them trouble, that we would stand with them. *Nobody gives us trouble,* the Lebanese man said, *these are good people here.* I thought of the man on the radio, and was less sure. Thank you, they said. God bless you, they said. May Allah bless them, too.

Yesterday we had a wonderful sermon from Tom Ferguson. One of the courses Tom teaches his undergraduates is a course in Islam. He led us through some things we needed to know about who Muslims are and who they are not. He used "You've Got To Be Taught" from *South Pacific.* PJ Nelson sang it at the 11:15; we had the original Lieutenant Cable on tape at 8 and 9:15. Interesting—Americans never want to talk about racism, but one of Broadway's most successful musicals ever was about exactly that. Tom led us to understand that we've all been "carefully taught," made us all want to unlearn some of the things that are part of the woodwork in our country. He made us want to start with ourselves and our community in doing what we can to heal our city, our nation and our world from what has happened.

Americans were confronted with the terrible shock that we could be ambushed right here in our own stores and offices and streets. Actually, Black Americans already knew that, already knew that it was not only possible but had happened many times, right here. Native Americans knew about it, too: you can just be having a normal day at home, cooking a meal at your fire with your children and you can look up and there's an army come to drive you a thousand miles from your ancestral land. Happens.

Americans of European descent should ask their African American and Native American and immigrant neighbors about living in this knowledge. About how they deal with it. They have a lot of experience. They have coped with this particular form of diabolical uncertainty for centuries. It is new only to Americans of the dominant culture. To everyone else, it's old news.

We'll Keep On Just Because We Have To

Everything gets old. Even things we care a great deal about cannot help but become something we're just used to, and this can be hard. Our recent tragedy is so immense that we feel terrible when we forget about it for a moment, when we do something normal and find ourselves enjoying it. How can I laugh at a time like this? But this normal moment is important.

For almost two weeks, everyone has wanted—needed—to be on the scene. We haven't known what to do with ourselves. We want to help, and we want to help directly. We have been willing to do anything. It has hurt some would-be volunteers' feelings to be told they are not needed, and some have expressed anger and bitterness about it.

As hard as the recovery effort is, as gripping as it is, as dramatic as it is, it is not the whole of the job before us. In fact, it is not even the hardest part. We will be left with something just as hard: to maintain the spirit of caring and commitment to the common life we love in this country after the crisis is over, after the last funeral, after the adrenalin is all used up. Afterwards, in an afterwards that could go on a long time, could provide other crises, more funerals. We are eager now, eager to help, eager to serve, eager to give and even to sacrifice. But we will be called upon to help and serve and give and sacrifice after all our eagerness has turned into something else: into impatience at how long the struggle will take, at the inconveniences it will cause in lives which may have known little inconvenience. We will be carrying the banner of our cause for a lot longer than we will want to carry it.

How will we find within ourselves the ability to do this difficult job? We will find it by becoming better acquainted with what love really is. We now think that love is a feeling, most of us. We are about to learn that love is, instead, a commitment. Our feelings propel us into it and sweeten our lives within it, but love is there even when the warm feelings aren't. Your mom may not have felt like getting up in the middle of the night with you when you had the stomach flu. She may have had the flu herself, and may have wanted nothing more than to sleep. But she got up anyway. Because you were her child and she loved you.

The firefighter and rescue workers and police officers didn't want to die. But they knew what their job was, and they did it. Just like your mom. We may not want to spend a number of years interrupting our lives, doing without things we're used to having, adjusting our actions to fit decisions we didn't make. But it is our job, as citizens, to do these things, and we will do them if we must. We have this choice about them: not whether or not to do them, but in what spiritual state we will do them. Will this struggle be characterized in our memories primarily as the story of our own deprivation and the unfairnesses heaped upon us? Or will we remember, instead, a time when we learned just how strong we really were? When we rose above our own self-absorption and approached something like nobility?

More Injured Than Thou

Something embarrassing is happening to my grief over the World Trade Center. It only happens when I'm not in New York, or when I'm talking to somebody who is not in New York. I first noticed what was going on with me last Monday, when I made a quick trip to Chicago.

Here is what it is: I find that I struggle with a highly irrational—and most unfair—anger against people who have not been as directly affected as we are. I find myself busily erecting a hierarchy of pain, in which we are the stars and everyone else just isn't doing his share. I found myself, in Chicago, impatient with the way things seemed to be going along in the usual way, angry at the Sears tower building because it was still standing. I could tell that I was different from the people there, that I was still shocky and they were not. When they said something kind to me about the bombing—which they all did—my eyes would fill with tears, without any warning. You are a mess, girl, I said to myself as I left the studio for the airport.

I became enraged the other night on the train: two women greeted one another with blood-curdling screams and I almost jumped out of my skin. *Stop that!* I said, before I could stop myself. They hadn't seen each other since the bombing and neither had known the fate of the other. Of course they screamed. Eminently understandable. I just couldn't take it. Embarrassing.

I worry about what I might do. This Sunday afternoon, I must head immediately down to somewhere near West Bat Dropping, Virginia to serve as chaplain to a diocesan clergy conference. Knowing this strange new self as I'm beginning to, I don't trust it. I fear what I might do when I'm down there. I must not be mean. I must not snap at people.

I must not feel sorry for myself, and I must not compare my city's pain with theirs.

Right.

I will do the best I can. We all will. Because we are all on edge, we will misstep occasionally, and we'd better cut ourselves and one another some slack when we do. Nobody is at his or her best every minute of every day when something like this happens.

Still an Emergency. Just a Different One.

Ernesto from the Seamen's Church Institute came by with Deacon Swanson. They were dropping off leftover food from Ground Zero—cases and cases. We can use it in the food pantry. And some leftover clothing, brand new men's t-shirts, dozens of them. All things no longer needed by the ongoing recovery operation, which looks like it will go on for a long time.

A young woman from across the street brought her dead boyfriend's computer. Could the church use it? She didn't have the heart to turn it on and go through the programs. I don't know what's on it, she said, but it's pretty new. Thank you.

A couple of firemen brought over large cans of fruits and vegetables, cases of them. We've got more, he said, and the Waldorf and other restaurants and chefs are doing all the food down there now. Good—we can use it for Thanksgiving Dinner.

The Dean of General Seminary sends a letter to all of us, telling us that they are officially off duty. Call Melvin at Trinity for instructions from now on. His letter is full of quiet pride at what his small community managed to do in the midst of this tragedy. And rightly so. His students will never forget this particular year in their seminary careers, and how it began. But they have course work to complete, and exams for which to prepare. They have to go forward.

The Seamen's Church Institute is also returning to its primary mission of service and advocacy work on behalf of seafarers. It has a long history of shoreside involvement in serving seafarers in our country's wars. This was not the first time unusual demands have been made on that unique institute, and it won't be the last.

Built to last, these old institutions: Trinity Church (1697), St. Paul's Chapel (1769), the Seamen's Church Institute (1834). Built to last, and more flexible than they appear. One thing age confers is experience, the certainty that hard times come and go, that God will always provide a will and a way to serve the people.

St. Clement's (1872), also, is no spring chicken. Like other old people and things, it is tough and wiry. We can catch what life throws at us. And life goes on, in our small corner of New York. We're glad to get the extra food and clothing, because the poor have remained in need of food and clothing all through our national tragedy and are expected to continue to get hungry for the foreseeable future. For life to get back to normal, while it may mean something different to many of us from what it meant before, means that the needs of humankind will continue to find their way to our door, and we cannot stop responding to them.

The rubble of Ground Zero looks different every time I go there, but it is also always the same: immense, beyond belief, shocking, overwhelming in the task it presents. There will come a time—not soon, but someday it will come—when that ground is flat again. Trees will grow on it, and people will walk on it, and laugh and play chess and argue and make up and fall in love. There will be buildings, I guess. There will come a time when nobody living will remember this terrible event.

But the ongoing needs of the poor will still be with us. God's people will always be called to serve. God will give them the strength to do so. That will not change.

You've Changed Something

"You know how I change my hair color when I get depressed?"

"Yeah."

"Well, I'm doing it now."

"I really liked the color you just got."

"It had too much blonde from the last time, so now I've just put some more brown in."

"Oh."

I know lots of people who change their hair when they change their moods. One man, frustrated at most of the people with whom he was working, came in one day—without a word—with stark white hair. I know a lady who dyes her hair blue at Christmastime every year. Seafarers I knew when I was on the waterfront would often change their faces—grow a mustache or a beard, shave one off, shave their heads, grow muttonchops whiskers—when they were at sea. I always thought it interesting that they did that. I used to wonder if they were trying to become someone else, so they wouldn't feel so alone when home was far away.

I remember many an early fall afternoon, at the hairdresser with my daughters and granddaughters: looking dubiously into the mirror at very curly permanent waves, at corkscrew curls that wouldn't last the night, at haircuts shorter than imagined beforehand, at hair that just didn't look as sophisticated on a 12-year-old as it did on the 19-year-old supermodel in the magazine. But it seemed that changing hair softened the anxiety about changing schools a little. My heart ached a little at the doubtful looks into the mirror; I also knew what it was to doubt my own worth, ability, and attractiveness in new situations.

Do you know something of that heartache? Do you feel it, sometimes, when you see someone fighting back the beginnings of a hurt you have known? We have seen so much hurt in recent weeks, hurt at a direct hit and hurt at the knowledge that someone else has been hit. No wonder we want to dye our hair: half of us doesn't even want to admit that any of this has happened, even now.

But it is this sympathetic ache that reminds us that we are still alive. Some New Yorkers were shocked by their own numbness in the midst of this tragedy: they felt nothing, cared about nothing, didn't want to watch the news or anything else. They felt half alive. And when the thaw came, they almost welcomed the tears that appeared at last. The ache means that love is present. We wouldn't have the ache if we didn't love. And we cannot love without the ache.

Murder No More

You may know that one of my great loves has been reading murder mysteries, that I have read one or two and sometimes even three a day for years, that I have been involved in the St. Clement's murder mystery swap ever since I came here. You may have read my story "Murder, She Read," in my last book, in which I speculate on my interest in such a morbid subject and also apprehend an Actual Criminal. For years, my ideal day has been spent in bed with a pile of murders. Invariably, I have emerged from all that carnage in a beatific state of mind, overflowing with the milk of human kindness toward all my fellow creatures. Go figure.

But you may not know that all of this changed abruptly on September 11. I haven't read a murder since then, nor have I desired to read one. I may never read one again, I don't know. Several of my favorite authors have brought out new ones since the 11th, and I have regarded them with indifference and even revulsion. I don't want to read fictional accounts of evil people doing horrible things to the innocent, even if the good guys do get them in the end. I don't want to read about sick people doing horrible things to others, either, even if they can't help it. Having evil become so real and come so close, off the page of a book and into our beloved city, is too much for me.

When it was fiction, I experienced crime as a thrilling but harmless release, a flight of imagination in which I took on the bravery and rage of others. When it's happening before my eyes, I don't need to see it in my imagination.

Saturday we went to a meeting—I know the only good meeting is a dead meeting, but this one was actually pretty good—and then to lunch at LeMonde. Then we went the Met to se the Breughel exhibition.

We had coffee and shared a scone in the Met coffee shop. We took the train home in time for *A Prairie Home Companion* and I read a book about the first geological map of England (more interesting than it sounds).

That may be my new ideal day.

St. Clement's was the elephants' graveyard of office machinery. Computers went there to die. This was where I began to try to use email. My thought was that I would send out little essays to my parishioners, as an aid to their spiritual lives. Sometimes it worked, and sometimes it didn't. The selection below represents one of those *times.*

Hello.

My email has been kaput for weeks. I am not ignoring you, nor have I ceased to like you.

My confidence in this medium, always tenuous, has sunk to a fairly solid conviction that it is much more likely not to work than to work.

My hostility to it, always latent, has blossomed, Taliban-like, into something a whole lot bigger than a breadbox.

I do not know if you will ever hear from me again on email. I will certainly try. But I have absolutely no confidence that it will work, and every reason, based on bitter experience, to believe that it will not.

bcc+

Seating Arrangements

"Actually, Robert and I are going to have Thanksgiving dinner separately after all," says Anna. "Neither one of us really wants to leave after a family dinner and go somewhere else, so we'll get together in the evening instead."

So I cross one body off the seating arrangement. I'm trying to get everyone at the same table, which seats twelve—a little snugly. But then I remember that Rosemary is coming and that she's bringing her boyfriend. Or maybe I'm wrong and she doesn't have that boyfriend anymore.

But then I think that Corinna's boyfriend may come. "No," she says, and doesn't elaborate. *Oka-ay*, I think and we're back to seven of us, unless Greg brings his mother out of the nursing home for the day, which maybe he will. Then we'll be eight.

"What are we going to have?" Rosie wants to know, although we have had the same menu for thanksgiving dinner for about fifty years. Madeline suggests potato salad which, as curator of Thanksgiving I reject as too summery. But then I think, Well, why not? What would be so awful about saving out a few potatoes and providing an alternative? I leave a message on their answering machine informing her of my change of heart. I do tell her it represents a momentous change, just so she doesn't get too used to making adjustments in tradition.

Young people who must struggle to combine a new love with old family loyalties. New loves not yet ready for family view. A lady whose life is nearing its end coming out one more time to sit next to her son and have him cut her turkey for her because her hands no longer work. A motherless young woman who feels we are her family on this day. When I was a child, we often had foreign intelligence officers at our

Thanksgiving table; Lieutenant Shimoda, I remember, who sat on the floor with me and showed me how to make origami birds. An officer from the Ukraine we called Mr. Ivanov. I don't remember how I knew this, but Ivanov was not his real name.

The first holiday of the season sets a tone: it's all about relationships. People. Whether you have one or many or none, you can't avoid thinking of them right now. Time is passing. Use each day to the fullest extent you can. You will not have it again. Take what joy there is and don't immediately cut it in half by moaning over not having more of it.

Peel Away

I knew I was overdosing on St. Clement's when I found myself tuning in to the news from the Afghan War in order to relax enough to get to sleep.

Even things we love can burn us out. Your children, your beloved—priceless gifts in your life, but a 24/7 diet doesn't work for most of us. At some point, you have to peel yourself away. You just have to. Whether you feel guilty or not. You'll get hurt if you don't.

That's what's happening down at Ground Zero. Although people are mad about it, it has to happen anyway: people have to peel themselves away. Emotion is not always the best guide in deciding things, and the people who feel the most powerful need to be there may really need, for their own safety and the safety of others, to get some distance.

Great advice. I struggle to follow it myself. Sometimes I succeed and sometimes I just don't. Sometimes the firefighters and the police and the rescue workers need someone else to gently—or maybe not so gently—peel them away from what they can't leave on their own. Maybe we all need that once in awhile.

On Sunday, December 19, I collapsed again. In church...again. This time it was during the announcements. Reminds me of a man I used to know who always said, "See you in church.... After the collection."

Nobody Is Indispensable

I will write my little meditation for the front of the Sunday bulletin here in my hospital bed, I thought, and then I can call it in to the voice mail and Paul Philpy can type it from there, like taking dictation. But, as I picked up my pen, the phone rang. Paul. He'd written one himself, he said, would I care to hear it?

It was great. It was better than the vague idea I had, so far, of what I might do. "Let's use yours," I said. "It's just right."

"Could somebody bring me a pad and a pen to the hospital?" I could write an eMo from the hospital and read it into PJ's voice mail and then she could put it up on the eMo group. But, when I called, PJ was mildly pleased at having already posted one herself. "I even got some comments," she said. And so I didn't write one.

I love to write the eMos. I love to write anything. But when you're ill, creative energy can be in short supply. I am amazed at how tired I am. If it were up to me, the eMos and the bulletin announcements would probably sound as weak as I feel.

Fortunately it's not up to me. St. Clement's is full of gifts, and by no means do they all reside in the rector. Many of us are actors and playwrights and directors, people who make their living from the power of words. More than the usual percentage of Clementines are theologically trained, well accustomed to conveying spiritual truth in terms that a secular world can understand. All of God's children are endowed with ability to hear God speak and to share God's word with others, lay people and ordained people alike.

"How are things?" I ask when I call in. "We're just keepin' on," says Clarence. Sounds good to me.

I'll be glad to get back when I am stronger. But I am not worried about you, Church. You are just fine.

Perhaps it has not been clear to you as you read these little snippets, but I was growing sicker and sicker throughout the fall of 2001. In this eMo, I share some bad news with the Clementines.

Dear Ones,

I am sorry you have not heard from me for so long. The email here at St. Clement's still does not work and, as I have said before, my expectations for its recovery are small.

You may also have heard that I have not been well. This is indeed true, and it has necessitated a decision about which you may also have heard through your various grapevines. With great sorrow, I have come to the conclusion that I must resign from St. Clement's. My resignation will be effective January 31st. St. Clement's requires the presence of a leader in good health and strength; I am, increasingly, not that person.

I think you know how hard this is for me. I have loved St. Clement's very much, and have put my heart and soul into leading it. But I have much respect for its many gifts and strengths, and know that God remains as leaders come and go.

We have two months together before I depart. Let's make them happy and meaningful ones. May the coming Christmas be our sweetest ever.

Faithfully,
bcc+

Love Well That Which Thou Must Leave Ere Long

The flowers in the window boxes did survive and thrive through the entire summer and into the fall, as Rebecca, Chris and I all bet they would. They only departed this past week, when we pulled them out and substituted an evergreen garland, threaded among the window boxes and looking something close to real. The church looks sweet and well-cared-for as the afternoon sun dips in the sky: its neat red trim, its window boxes full of green, the lights shining through the stained glass—the windows in my office.

It is the most beautiful office I have ever had, and among the most beautiful I have ever seen. Visitors always comment on its peaceful feeling, its dark wood, the beautiful rich color of the walls, the warmth of the candles that usually burn there.

It is hard to believe that soon it will no longer be mine. That someday fairly soon it will be someone else's. It is hard for me to believe that I will actually leave here soon, that the destinies that have been intertwined for almost six years will part company. Hard, and painful as well. I imagine no longer being part of the worship we have shared and the service we have offered, and I am sad.

Will everyone be all right? Will we make it, St. Clement's and I, separated from each other? Of course we will. I will recover my health, and St. Clement's will continue its work and witness. That which is of God will continue. And it is also true that love shared between the children of God never dies. Love never ends, the apostle Paul says. Friendship endures.

At funerals, Lee Winston often sang a Daryl Curry song. He even sang it at his own funeral, on a recording. It's called "Families Continue." Now, of course, we know that death and separation interrupt families all the time; three thousand families are struggling through the first holiday season without a dear one from the WTC bombing alone. So the lives do not continue, not as they were. But that which made the family, the love that bound and continues to bind it together—that goes on. It's something we will never lose, no matter what. Because it's love, and love comes from the heart of God.

Learning to Fail

The idea was that I would make pralines this morning before leaving for St. Clement's at midday. They don't require as much standing as many other sweet things, and my pralines are pretty good, if I do say so myself.

Today, however, I used a different recipe. This one was called "Southern Pralines," which sounded much more authentic, and it also yielded more candies, so they would go farther as gifts. Had I reflected on that fact, I might not have been so surprised when the saucepan I have always used for pralines proved insufficient to the new amount. Sugar mixtures are notorious for boiling up extravagantly and swiftly, and for being wretched to clean up: the sugar hardens to a rocklike finish on the surface of the stove and the burners, and you have to take the whole thing apart. And you haven't even gotten to the pans yet. I poured the over-boiling pralines into a larger pan. This pan was also inadequate; I kept it on the heat for as long as I could and then, unable to face another boil-over, tossed in the butter and hoped for the best. This act prevented the mixture from ever reaching the softball stage, a term known to candy makers and the rest of you just never mind.

You beat the pralines for only a minute or two, and they ordinarily become stiff enough that you can drop them onto waxed paper into the lovely patties we all think of when we think of pralines. I beat for much longer than should have been necessary, but the liquid remained discouragingly thin. I dropped a couple of dozen on the waxed paper, but even I could see that these things were never, ever going to be hard enough to pick up and eat.

So we have two vessels of praline ice cream topping in our refrigerator that we didn't have before. I will try the pralines again as soon as I can find a washtub to cook them in.

For some reason I wasn't frantic. *What the hell,* I said to myself. Q likes ice cream. I like ice cream, although I can't eat it anymore. I'll make some more pralines someday soon. Or maybe some year soon.

I hate to fail. Hate it, hate it, hate it. But it usually doesn't make the big difference in human affairs that it feels like to me whenever I fail. It just happens and then life goes on and I live with whatever fallout there is. Maybe one day I'll come to enjoy it as the lesson it is.

Then I can do it all the time....

Mothered by Others

More cooking news: yesterday the ladies of the Quiet Hour Club came to my house for their Christmas meeting. The club dates from 1895. I joined 22 years ago in 1981—twenty years the junior of the youngest member of Quiet Hour.

Twenty years later, I am more in the middle. There are one or two members who may be younger than I am by a year or two. There is now one Jewish member; I wondered, as we sang Christmas carols at the end of the meeting, how she was handling it. I exchanged a raised eyebrow with her and she shrugged and smiled, shaking her head. "Whatever" is what that meant. But the routine is always exactly the same: a scrumptious tea table in our dining room, with scrumptious home-made cookies and candies and my mother's and Q's mother's tea service and all the pretty flowered cups and saucers my mother left me.

Spritz cookies were to be among the delicacies. I had a "spell" during the mixing of the cookie dough, though, necessitating a quick lie-down. By the time I came to, I had forgotten whether or not I had doubled the recipe. I concluded that I had not, and put in the normal amount of flour. But, lo: it turned out that I had doubled the butter, so the cookies sheet emerged not with neat rows of identical plump poinsettias but completely covered with a lacy layer of paper thin cookie. Oh, dear.

Thinking quickly, I cut them into several dozen small square cracker-shaped things. I tasted one and it was delicious—fine. Still not enough cookies, and the table looked a little skimpy to me. I was still too weak to even think about another batch of something, so I cut into the fruitcake Anna and I made last week. It was still drunk, quite unable either to speak or stand, having soaked in bourbon for the past four days, but it was delicious. Fine.

Three ladies came early. In a sense, they have watched me grow up: I was 29 when I came to serve their church, my first position as a priest, and they were all old enough to be my mother. They took one look at me and fell to work: arranging the teapots and the cups, brewing the coffee, deploying the cookies on beautiful plates, filling the cream pitchers, placing the chairs. I sat in one of the chairs and watched. They did the tea, and then they did the cleanup. I sat in the chair.

During the tea, the ladies exclaimed over the deliciousness of the lacy former spritz cookies, the drunken fruitcake, the lemon bars, the jam thumbprints. I sat in a chair and signed books for peoples' Christmas presents. Afterwards, Mary Jones stayed with me because she was afraid to leave me alone—Q was away. They think I am more fragile than I am, or maybe I think I am less fragile than I am. I am not sure yet. She sat and addressed her Christmas cards while I lay on the other couch and slept. At suppertime she brought me come wonderful soup she had made. Delicious. I went back to sleep.

My mother has been dead for 21 years. Even now, I think of her every day. She meant so many comforts to me, ways in which I could stop for breath and reassurance, care that was loving and had nothing at all to do with the success or failure of whatever I was in the midst of accomplishing. But her life in the Kingdom of Heaven means that others appear in this life to do the things she did and be the things she was. None of us is irreplaceable, no matter how much love has bound us together for a season in a common journey.

Snow and Ice Glorify the Lord

Buffalo is under seven feet of snow. They don't mind much: the first few feet are the hardest, and after that it doesn't make much difference. Atlanta, on the other hand, has closed schools and all businesses and state offices for its five inches. Three people have crashed their cars and died as a result—you don't learn much about driving in snow in Atlanta. Now it's moving into the Carolinas, where snow is always something of a shock, even though it does snow a little every year.

I remember a wonderful picture in the *Times*, years ago: snow had fallen in Rome, and people were walking through the *Piazza del Populo* with their umbrellas, entranced by this rarity.

When's the earliest it's snowed here, I asked a new friend when I moved to Ithaca. "Well," she said, "I don't think we've ever had snow in August. But we've had it in every other month."

But it is my home state that outdistances everyone in terms of snow and cold. It is routinely 30–40 degrees below zero in Minnesota, and in International Falls it's not unusual for it to go to fifty below. Again, the first few degrees below zero are the hardest; after that, who cares? A cat once came to us out of the cold and went to live in our basement. After a few days, her tail and ears had fallen off. She got to us just in time, I'd say, while she still had a head and paws.

We may get some snow this weekend. I hope so. I hope we get the kind that makes everybody just take the day off. There is nothing nicer than being inside when it's snowing outside, or than venturing forth into snow that makes this noisy city almost silent.

Somehow, the psalmist knew about snow. They don't have much in the Holy Land, but I guess they have a little. Enough to know about it. He orders it to praise the Lord—*Ice and snow, glorify the Lord!* and it does, when it shrouds the earth in beauty and stops time for a little while.

Positively Negative

I flunked my stress test this morning. I hate to fail. They cushion the blow in medical testing by the clever use of language: "Well, your test is positive," the doctor said, as we peered together at a video of my heart pumping away. "Positive" is such a—well, positive word. Sounds like you've done something well. But you haven't, not when it's about a medical test. It means you do indeed have whatever annoying thing you were hoping you didn't have.

"This isn't very bad, though," he continued as the different heart videos kept pumping away on the screen. Several valves opened and shut together, but one of them was out of step with the others. But just a *little* off, sort of like a musical piece Charles Ives might have written. "Dr. Leber will call you in a few days."

Whatever. I am tired of Dr. Leber. I am tired of every last one of his colleagues. It would be a pleasure never to see any of them again. How mean of me—none of them have ever been anything but kind, even when they were doing something awful to a middle-aged woman in a skimpy cotton robe that left her backside only precariously covered, when it was covered at all.

The things that help us don't always feel very helpful at the time. You can't always go with how something feels right at this particular moment in evaluating it. Few good things in life happen with ease, and sometimes health is hard to regain.

So is faith, sometimes. The beginnings of a new spiritual practice can feel foreign and uncomfortable. "I hate this prayer book—everybody here knows what page we're on but me." "I'm trying to use centering prayer, but I keep thinking about the laundry I haven't done." "I try to pray for my enemies, but all I do is get mad and forget all about prayer."

But even the difficulty beginning of a life in faith is still a beginning, and the beginning of a good thing is always good.

The Poor Were Here Before Starbucks

The doorbell has been ringing all morning. Al-Anon members arriving and departing, techies from the last show coming in and out with lighting equipment, people bringing thrift shop donations, people wanting to know when the food pantry opens, people just wanting to say hello. St. Clement's is not a place for people who need a lot of silence. The phone's been busy, too, but in a strange way: you pick it up and you hear a beep and then—nothing. What are those, anyway? Junk faxes? Terrorists? Who knows.

The last of the donated turkey from Thanksgiving was consumed with relish at the confirmation dinner Wednesday. At least, I think it's the last. If we look in every freezer, we will probably find another one. What a miracle these turkeys are: we begin the week of Thanksgiving dinner with nothing on hand and we end it overflowing with turkey and cans of cranberry sauce and God knows what—enough, and more than enough. Sometimes, Food for Survival (our primary food pantry supplier) has an unexpected windfall of fresh fruit or vegetables. It's never a small windfall—it's a whole truck farm. After the food pantry people have taken their fill, there are still cartons and cartons of apples, carrots, onions, tomatoes, whatever it is, Charles and whoever else is around set up shop on the sidewalk and give away produce to surprised passers-by.

This is fast becoming something other than a poor neighborhood. Folks who have been here awhile remember how poor it was, and how hard life was for the families that lived here. Now there are boutiques and four-dollar cups of coffee here, but there are still a lot of people in need.

I believe that nothing is more important for the poor to see than images of God's abundance. Piles of fruit there for the taking. A hearty welcome at the door. A gorgeous Thanksgiving or Christmas dinner table waiting for the diners to arrive, that cup of coffee accompanied by a smile. God relies on people to show the divine abundance—you can, indeed, see God in a beautiful sunset, but you are less likely to look if your stomach is empty and likely to remain so.

I am leaving you soon. Please do not forget how much the world that passes by our doors and sometimes comes in needs to see God's abundant love. Even if you yourself are feeling poor and in want, even if you're feeling cross and underappreciated, even if you are angry at somebody, please stop and remember how healing a thing it is to be a part of giving in the name of Christ.

Light Shines in the Darkness

New York City is defined by light.

In its first generations, its only light was the small amount that spilled out from between closed shutters in the windows of the tiny houses. Little boys were hired to go before pedestrians with lighted torches, so they wouldn't fall into a ditch or lose their way. Soon, oil lamps appeared and with them, the civic figure of the lamplighter, who daily climbed the ladder to fill each lamp with oil and daily climbed again to light it at dusk.

The mid-19th century brought gas lamps, each haloed with a golden sphere. And then, toward the turn of the 20th century, amazing electric lights, casting more light farther than ever before. New York light was amazing: visitors from other countries commented on the myriad windows of the taller and taller buildings. And, in the 20th century, neon: light that curved and moved in brilliant arcs of color. We looked to the lights to satisfy our longings—for the news, to observe the New Year, to know we were in New York.

Most small children are afraid of the dark. In the dark, you feel alone. Your furniture looks larger. But New York City provides its own night light: just crack the curtain a bit, and a sliver of light keeps you company in the dark. It may be that it is not only small children who fear the dark. Perhaps we all fear darkness of some kind or other, darkness outside or darkness within ourselves. But at Christmas, we remember: the light shines in the darkness, and the darkness has not overcome it. In the dark or in the light, God is with us. And we are not afraid.

Keep It Simple

Joan arrives to sign paychecks and finds me weeping over the email. “Wouldn’t you like to go out for some coffee and give yourself a break?” she asks cautiously, and I nod mutely, unable to trust myself to speak. Off we go to Starbucks which, like email, is a somewhat more complicated experience than it needs to be, requiring patrons to choose among the aromatic products of various coffee-producing tropical countries, different grinds of coffee and types of milk, discern the probable meaning of Italian words as applied to cup sizes, and lie in wait to pounce on an available table, like a suburban minivan driver in a shopping mall parking lot.

But we do snag one. I pour out my heart about the email in little bits: how much I hate being the only person in North America who has a hard time with it, how much a failure I feel about this lack of ability along with all my other faults, like not knowing how to change the cartridge on the copy machine without spilling inky black powder all over everything and having a hard time with an adding machine (I get a different total every time, no matter how many times I add) and not being able to remember what people who are good at technical tasks tell me about how to do all these things. “Oh, it’s easy,” they say, “you just download the upflange on the megabyte, burn it into a CD-ROM, drop it onto a double-beat floppy and save it as a draft in your zip. Then you attach what you’re sending—save it in a few different ways just in case—and send it. As long as you’ve got 40 or 50K, it’ll be fine.” It never is.

Sometimes I think time has passed me by. That a parish priest really needs to be a computer adept. That is probably true. But if time is really passing me by, I wish it would also leave me alone. Instead, I find myself chained to technologies I cannot use or comprehend. I long for paper, for ink on paper that, when read, communicates ideas. I long for communication that is a little less than instantaneous, for the considered words that a slower life necessitates. For humor that does not have to signal itself with a <g>. If something's really that funny, we probably don't have to be told.

But then Joan mentions her father, and his failing health. I remember that her mom died just a year ago, and I am on familiar ground again. However prompt and efficient email makes life, it will never substitute for the presence of another human being, someone with a heartbeat and a bloodstream and a memory of the death of her own parents that, years later, can still bring tears to the eyes.

For heaven's sake, get yourselves a priest who can send an email without passing out. But never forget that, whatever else we can't do, Christ's love is sent through human beings and it is our sacred calling—lay and ordained—to bring it to the world.

II

From the Geranium Farm

A Volunteer Tomato

Many of the geraniums came inside to spend the winter, including the grandmother of them all, from whose thick woody stem have come dozens of colorful descendants, rooted first in glasses of water and then little pots of Q's magic compost. Four geraniums are in the kitchen window, which gets a lot of sun, and two or three are upstairs, where sunlight is also quite good. They have obliged our hospitality by blooming throughout the fall and winter, especially those in the kitchen. Visitors compliment the profusion of blooms in the kitchen, and I glow with pride, as if I had something to do with it.

But three months ago I noticed a tomato—a tomato!—sprouting alongside one of the pink geraniums. What are you doing here, I growled, but I knew. That's the thing about compost: it's a combination of rotted food, leaves and other rotting stuff, including the occasional tomato. In the rich medium it produces once earthworms have run it through their digestive systems—"Ahh, worm turds!" Q always says when he shows me a shovelful, "Isn't that beautiful?"—the seeds in a discarded tomato cannot help but spring to life, and now one was coming up in my geranium farm. I watched it for a few weeks.

I should have smothered it in its cradle, but Q is as loving with his tomatoes as I am with my geraniums, so I let it be. Before long, it was a foot tall, and had blossoms. Now it's two feet, and wants to shade all my geraniums. Now, wait a minute. I was here first.

It is as if I have not spoken. "It's a *volunteer*," Q says, as if that settled it. A volunteer, like hospital volunteers and Thanksgiving dinner volunteers and Ground Zero volunteers. Well, maybe. I continue to let it grow—a volunteer, I cannot interrupt it now, and even I must accord the unexpected tomato plant a grudging respect. It had no obligation to come here, and was not expected, but here it is.

Ah, people will come into your life and help you when you don't want help. You will either chase them away and carry on as before, or you will cock your head to one side and look at them and think, "Well, maybe." If you do the first, you will have full control. If you do the second, you will open your life to a surprise. Maybe a good one and maybe a bad one. If that tomato plant shades my geraniums out of blooming, we're going to have a talk. But if we have both bright geranium blooms and an actual tomato, it will be spectacular.

Don't Look at Me. Look at What I See.

I'm writing a painful essay, I told my editor in an email. *I think it's going to be really good.* Not too painful, I hope, she wrote back cautiously.

Writing isn't good just because it's confessional. That's the horrid mistake of daytime TV—people think that the simple awfulness of spilling their guts is moving. It's usually not—it's usually just appalling. There's more to writing than just vomiting your life out on the page. The same is true of preaching: your experience can furnish wonderful points of contact with your people, but it takes more than just sharing your secrets with them. If all you want to do is share your secrets, call a best friend or find a therapist.

But there are moments in life that are sufficiently rich in the presence of God, and sufficiently common to all people in some important aspect of them, that they will edify, if planted with skill. We're all called to be honest. Some of us are called to share the fruits of our honesty in a way that leads to grace.

This needs fleshing out a little, I think, Anna writes. She is right. *Maybe you should put it aside and come back to it in a day or two.* Good idea. Painful things often cannot be digested at one sitting: I find that I become superficial and glib if I try to face them down for too long a time at once.

So it isn't that my new essay is painful that will make it good, if it should happen to become good. What will make it good is that people will see in it something they have seen before, something they recognize. More than seeing me in the story, they will, instead, see what I *see.* If I can usher them into the story themselves with sufficient potency that it feels as autobiographical to them as it does to me, then God can speak to them in it as s/he speaks to me. Each of us is unique. None of us have precisely the same experiences. But we are all the same species, and we recognize ourselves in each other.

I Remember Mama

Monday—gray, rainy, back to work, back to the things you may have just shoved aside in order to do something for Mother's Day.

Some people went to see their Moms. They went to lovely, well-kept family homes or oddly new senior citizen residences. They went to nursing homes. They went to cemeteries. Or they had nowhere to go.

Their mothers were glad to see them. They took their mothers out to lunch. Or the visit brought up old difficulties, and the lunch ended in a fight. Again. Or their mothers weren't quite sure who they were and tried to hide it. Or their mothers weren't able to speak or to move, or even open their eyes. Or their mothers were gone from this world and lived in another one, a better one.

After the visit, they were happy. Or they were full of regret at the passing of time. Or they were sorry for their mothers, or glad to be their children. Or they were angry. Or they wondered about heaven and what it was like.

They admire their mothers. Or they're ashamed of them. They wish their mothers would stop lecturing them now they're adults, or they still wish their mothers would pay some attention to them. They wish they could please them. Or they wish their mothers were still alive.

They catch sight of themselves in the mirror and think for a minute that it's their mother looking back. They are nothing like her. They are exactly like her. She would be angry if she really knew who they were. She would be proud.

And now, this morning, the web of mixed feelings and longings lifts. It's time to work now. It's grown-up time. This is the present—it's not your childhood, not a never-never land of love that never was, not an old battleground still crying out for blood. Whoever she is, whoever she was, we are now the ones who run our lives and make them work. She stands in the doorway and waves good-bye, looks up from her hospital bed and smiles a little, closes her eyes for the last time, hangs up the phone. Good-bye, Mama.

You've Got Mail

The mail arrives. Ah, good—an actual letter. It turns out to be a note from Bobby Hecht at St. Clement's. He sent me a service bulletin to admire. He also sends me a cartoon he's made out of clip art: he has added a clerical collar to the line drawing of an anonymous office worker bending calmly over her computer keyboard. I can tell it's supposed to be me, because he has also added curse words.

I was famous at St. Clement's for not being able to use a computer. People would show me how to do something and I would get it. Then, when I would try on my own, nothing worked. Every time I successfully sent email represented about a dozen attempts that failed. Suggestions that I email people began to sound to me like acts of aggression.

After a two-month breathing spell at home, I got up the nerve to call Gateway. There a nice young man walked me through the purchase of a modest array of gear that would do what I needed to do. In just a few days, the boxes arrived, inexplicably patterned like the hide of a Holstein cow. I unpacked them and installed it myself. I set up my user name and my email account. I only had to call my 12-year-old granddaughter a few times.

Now I email all the time. I submit manuscripts through the ether. I arrange to tape a TV show with people I've never met; how will I know them when it's time to begin? I guess they'll be the ones with the cameras.

Anna flashes me a little message four or five times on a day I am writing at home. They read like e.e.cummings poems: no caps, not much in the way of periods or commas, either. I flash back. It's sort of like the idle chitchat of two people working in the same room.

I criticized it when I couldn't do it. I felt it was alienating and distancing, that the intimacy it fostered was fraudulent. But now I'm not so sure. Now I can't help but think it's nice. It's not just like personal contact, but its good contact. At 1:00 a.m. my aching leg wakes me up, and I decide to use the time to catch up on some work. I see that Brad has sent me an email with some articles. I send one back. He replies instantly, scolding me for being awake. Look who's talking. What is Brad, a vampire? I ask Bobby. Bobby says yes, he is. And look who's talking.

The long and short of email is that people need to connect. If it's in person, that's the best: a computer doesn't have an epidermis, and you definitely miss that. But if it's not, anything is better than nothing. A lot better. In former centuries, before telephones, all communication over distances took place by letter. People had been dead for months before their families heard about it. Wars were begun and ended and people didn't find out for weeks. Today I check some news sites about the terrible events in the Holy Land; I know about it while it's happening.

I don't know if life was kinder then. I doubt it. It was slower, but it was a 17-century figure who characterized the lives of most people as "nasty, poor, brutish and short." Whatever it was like, we can't go back there. History only goes forward. Here I sit, sending almost-daily bits of fluff to people I love but seldom see. They will delete or read: their choice. But at least we have the chance to connect.

Ora et Labora

Don't your Sims need a vacation? the ad said. My granddaughter has all the Sims computer games, including Sims Vacation, which I just got her. The Sims are virtual people whose lives you control in the game: they get jobs, lose jobs, have fires in their kitchens, get married. Madeline is absorbed in them for hours at a time.

I have become so intrigued by the Sims that I dreamed about them. In my dream, they were real: tiny little beings that I had made and set out on their lives. Kind of like God. But my dream turned into a nightmare: I overheard two of my creations planning to build a large church, and awoke my husband with my cries of panic.

Honest. I wouldn't make this up.

I guess it means I am nowhere near ready to resume parish ministry. I guess it means that my current lifestyle is the right one for now, and that I fear that the church may somehow catch me and convince me to abandon it too soon. It is difficult for me to resist feelings of obligation and guilt in this new freelance life of mine: now that I am feeling better, I begin to feel that I should be working myself to death somewhere. But all I would do if I yielded to that feeling would be to work myself to death, and my desire not to die is why I made this momentous change.

Writing *is* work. So is speaking in public. So is doing spiritual direction. So are eMos. All of these things are things I do well, and all are things that feed my soul. We have a responsibility, I think, to use the gifts God gave us to the fullest extent possible. By the time we grow up, we'd better be in a position to use our gifts in what we do for a living. If we don't do that, we're frustrated and angry all the time.

What about folks who lose their jobs? And are compelled by economic pressure to take work that *doesn't* feed their souls at all? *I'm just doing this theatre thing until I can find a position in the restaurant industry*, Cynthia used to say, deadpan. If you are one whose work is deadening rather than life-giving to you, there are some spiritual truths to remember:

1) There is a nobility in doing work you dislike for the sake of a higher good. Your family's survival is one of those higher goods. So is your own. There is no shame in doing a job you don't like and doing it well. It takes guts.
2) There is always the hope that your strong desires and your work can come closer together. God has a destiny for you, and your God-given destiny is never to live a life without meaning. So stay tuned, and watch for signs.
3) Even a job you adore can be a pain in the butt.

The God of the Garden

Do you have a rake? Madeline wanted to know. *We're weeding the garden.*

That was all I needed to hear. "I'll be right over," I said, although I had not been invited. There they were, pulling weeds out of the tiny plot of outside their condominium door.

"I'm not sure what's a weed and what's not," Corinna says. Everything is, basically, except a few tulips, and soon we are rewarded with a nice little expanse of bare, crumbly earth.

"Don't we need to get all the dried leaves and stuff out?" Madeline likes order.

"Nah," I say, "just blend them right in. They'll rot." Madeline looks pained. The soil is dark and good from having been "improved" last year with Q's compost, a rich mixture of rotted food and worm turds. The worms eat the garbage and it comes out their other ends. I tell Madeline about the worm turds and she laughs. I've found that everybody laughs when you bring up worm turds, and why not? We plant a few daisies. Today I will bring some lily-of-the-valley.

Is there anything better than a garden as a metaphor for God's love? Is there a metaphor more diverse than this one—the garden, in which things long-buried and seemingly dead come to green life and then to flower after their long, cold sleep; the garbage of life turned into rich nourishment through the ministry of a simple creature many people find disgusting.

"How can you touch them? They're so slimy," Madeline says about the worms.

"They probably feel the same way about us," I tell her. "They probably say "Eeeuw, how can you let them touch you? They're so dry!" She smiles again.

In a garden, everything has a turn. You can have beauty all year long, but you can't have the same *kind* of beauty all the time: plants have their seasons of bloom, and when it is over, we all have to go on. And something else comes into flower.

Different plants have different gifts. The ones that crave shade can't make it in full sun. The sunny ones won't flower if they're under a tree. Their diversity must be respected, or you won't have a lovely garden. You'll have a lumpy group of sullen plants that are not living up to their potential. Does this sound familiar?

And a garden often asks for our participation. God waters it from heaven, but sometimes it needs some help from us. We can make a difference in a garden just by seeing what it needs and taking some action.

And in the end, it is a joy to behold—God's great goodness given living form, in color of leaf and bloom, in cheek-by-jowl harmony among the different plant souls, a community of the living and the dead, of life emerging from decay. Praise to the God of the gardener and of the worm, of the rose and the rotted half-grapefruit, praise to the God of the rake and the sweet rains of spring.

Only One Sermon

I never got to meet Martin Luther King or Mother Theresa. I was too late for Gandhi. But Desmond Tutu is my contemporary, and he is still alive. I finally got to hear him in an extended way at the spirituality summit at the Kanuga Center in North Carolina.

As a speaker, he is like a mischievous child: cackling with laughter at things he might have cried about if he were someone else, draining all the poison out of the world's sorrows with his own unique combination of love and satire. *I only have one sermon,* he said last Thursday, *so if you hear that I'm to be the preacher, you needn't come.*

His one sermon is that God love us. That's it, really. Just that God loves us. Just that, as he put it, *If we really understood how much God loves us, we'd all genuflect before one another in awe.* That's a sight I'd walk more than a mile to see. Maybe I'd walk a whole life. *And we don't have to do a single thing. God just loves us.*

Like other great souls, Bishop Tutu doesn't know that he is special in any way. He thinks he's normal. Maybe he really is normal: maybe people like Desmond Tutu and Mohandas Gandhi are placed here among us to show us what normal is, what the human being is like when everything that *could* be active in the soul *is* awake and working. Perhaps we are normally great souls ourselves, and these people walk with us a while to remind us of what we really are. I think that must be so, because they change so many lives. They set captives free, not just a few captives, but millions of them.

I was thinking of these things on a walk—the conference center is in the lovely mountains of western North Carolina and it is a walker's paradise. I was alone, loving the flowers and the trees and the birds, when I looked further along the trail and saw that Sister Mary Martha was coming toward me. We had talked of going for a walk together earlier that day, and now here she was. *There are some lovely lady's slippers back there,* she said, and we went to find them.

Lady's slippers—I had been looking at a nursery catalogue before coming to North Carolina. They had lady's slipper for sale—at a hundred dollars a plant. A hundred dollars! *Damn well better grow*, I thought as I turned the page. The ad said that there were a limited number of lady's slipper plants available, so people should order soon. By now, yuppie gentleman farmers have snapped up all the lady's slippers, I'm sure.

Sister Mary Martha and I went back along the path. There were the lady's slippers—several exquisite plants, their golden-rosy blooms bending modestly toward the earth, unaware of their beauty. They grow wild in North Carolina, and in many woodlands of the rural south. They grow wild—nobody has to give anybody else a hundred dollars to see them. Nobody has to do a single thing. They are just there, for the beauty of it, because it is what they naturally do.

I only have one sermon, says the diminutive great soul. *God loves us.*

The Sickness Unto Death

Today I read from my work at a meeting of clergy colleagues. I chose an excerpt from a new book I am working on, which will deal with how a person of faith approaches depression. I use myself, as always, as something to examine, but I will also be looking at other people: Søren Kierkegaard, maybe, and Simone Weil, and the poet William Cowper, and George Herbert, who lay on the floor of his tiny church and wept throughout the night before he was to take charge of it, convinced he would not prove to be a faithful servant. Been there.

I will also talk of people who are not famous, people of faith who are visited, only once or every now and then, by the dark demon who visits me. Is the time spent in something close to despair—or something well over the edge of it—just time lost? Is there something to be found in that darkness? Can it instruct? Stay tuned.

My colleagues knew something of what I read. Everybody does: you don't have to have a clinical diagnosis to know what it is to be bone-weary and fed up with yourself. The life of faith can be a hard life: it insists on taking every minute as a potential moment in which God acts, and therefore every moment must be examined carefully as to one's motivation, stated and unstated, and one's responses, from the truly shabby to the somewhat noble. Some of our moments aren't very pretty.

I know, because people have told me, that the depressed differ from one another. For some of them, God is just absent—there is no sense of God, no sign of God, even no interest in God—just nothing. For others, God is all *too* present, a stern taskmaster who can never be satisfied. For some, God is whimsical and cruel, dispensing joy and suffering with seeming indifference. And they can never answer back, for the simple reason that God is bigger than they are.

For me, it was not like that. For me, God was loving. Love itself. Heaven was vivid and open to all. But I was not in it, and could not be in it. I believed in God all right; it was myself I didn't believe in. It was indescribably lonely.

The tradition was all there was to hang on to. I simply knew, because I had been told, that God was merciful and welcomed everyone, and that it didn't make sense that this wouldn't apply to me, alone among all God's children. The logic of this was tepid comfort at best, but it was logic. I lurked beside it until my feelings could catch up with its truth. It took a while: some major life changes and some time.

I want to write this book because many, if not most, of the most worthwhile people I have known have battled depression at one time or another in their lives. Perhaps people of faith will find themselves in its pages and understand that nothing lasts forever, not joy but also not pain. Tomorrow will always come. And, on the day when it doesn't, that'll be all right, too, because we'll be home at last.

Who Is This, Really?

Notice anything new?

Perhaps not. You probably can't see my speedy new DSL line, which—naturally—I installed myself. I am not exactly sure what its benefits will be, other than the major one: I can talk on the phone while sending eMos. And, I understand, I don't have to wait to go online. I'm online all the time.

Today the computer people called just to see how I was doing. That was thoughtful. Judging by the accent at the other end of the line, the young woman was calling from somewhere in the South. By the way, she asked, did I want to extend my service plan with Gateway? She went on to tell me about viruses and how Gateway would redo my hard drive for nothing if I had a service contract and a virus at the same time. She scared me silly—I didn't realize you get viruses from email. I thought it was the night air. That's what my mother always said.

The thought crossed my mind—as I read her the credit card number (she explained that this was the really long number on the front of my card)—that she herself, this nice little southern girl, might be a scam artist. That she's not from Gateway at all, that she's sitting in some squalid motel room in Indiana with her no-account boyfriend, ordering Chinese food, getting peoples' credit card numbers, and buying stuff. Chinese food and other stuff. I decided to test her—I asked her when I got my computer. She found my order date and estimated a delivery date. She seemed so confused but so pleasant that I decided she can't be a thief. She'd be unemployed if she were.

Viruses...thieves from the South, by way of Indiana? Anything is possible with computers. We can get scammed by people we will never meet.

But, on the other hand, an instant message buddy of mine just told me she'd met a new love on line. And then they met in person. And it's just as lovely. And tomorrow stretches out in front of them, just as it does when people meet each other in the old way. Oh, brave new world, plunked down right in the middle of the old one. It makes you want to get up in the morning just to see what new things have arrived while you were asleep.

All the World Loves a Crone

"I may be a crone now," I whisper to my husband over breakfast. He raises an eyebrow inquiringly.

"I wouldn't have described you that way," he says.

"No," I go on, still whispering. I don't know why I'm whispering. Nobody is home but us. "All I have to do is not bleed for nine more months and I'm a crone."

"Is that okay?"

"It is now." I am reading an upbeat book about menopause. Menopausal women are crones, and a crone is a good thing, it says in the book. A crone is a wise old woman whose childrearing life is behind her. It recommends various herbal concoctions for what ails menopausal women, and makes it all sound like an exclusive club anybody with any sense would be eager to join. It suggests a ceremony on the night of the first full moon after thirteen consecutive months without a menstrual period have passed, something you do with fire and sage. I am not a night person.

I'm a team player, but there are downsides to being a crone. I walk like a crab when I first get out of bed. Or even when I arise from a chair. Once I get going, I'm fine, but the first few steps are painful indeed. Sometimes my hip and leg hurt when I'm not even moving; sometimes they wake me up at night. I remember an old lady telling me once about being awakened at night by her arthritis and walking back and forth in the dark. Now it's happening to me. Small world. Short life.

Then there is the asymmetry: one eyelid is more pleated than the other. Now, who let *that* happen? Wouldn't you think they'd sag on more or less the same timetable, since both eyelids are the same age? At the nail place I see a woman with a face-lift she must profoundly regret: her skin is stretched so tightly over her bones that she looks like a puppet. I didn't see her smile the whole time I was there. I'm not sure she can. I look with new fondness at my uneven eyelids when I get home. *Oh, well.*

And varicose veins in only one leg—how odd. Not that I'm complaining.

The crone in the menopause book is so full of serenity and wisdom you want to slap her. It says her obligations are behind her and people can come and see her for advice and that other peoples' problems don't bother her. They sure bother me. I don't know many people for whom that detachment is consistently there; obligations have a way of coming back just when you thought they were finished. But maybe they're not obligations. Maybe I just think they are. A true crone would know the difference.

The menopause book says you should allow your body to gain ten pounds just in case. Allow? My body never even asks. It just goes right ahead. In case of what? In case I start to become a spidery little being, matchlike of wrist and ankle, blue veins roping under transparent skin with no cushion of softness around them, none around my swollen joints. Oh. I am six feet tall. Or was until I started to shrink. Still, there must be limits to how much a person can shrink. Some of us will just never be spidery.

We might have known that being old would become desirable once the baby boomers got old—chic always follows the money. But the generation of kids now in high school is, I hear, even larger, which means that pretty soon the money is going to leave us high and dry. We won't be seeing a moment in advertising when hip old people in designer jeans are present in anything but an occasional moment of photographic patronizing, a rare pat on the head—the young, slim, fit body will continue to rebuke us all from the pages of magazines.

The crone in the book disapproves of plastic surgery. Why am I not surprised? She doesn't think we should donate the fat from our own derrières to fill in our crow's-feet. I say she should mind her own business. To each her own—her own derrière (or his!) and her own crow's feet.

The crone in the book finishes a chapter and subsides into a nap. She says we should just take a nap whenever we feel like it. Good idea. Most people would love to do that—you're reading this after lunch, probably, a fine time for a nap if ever there was one. But you probably are not at liberty to indulge just now. Most of us get our crone bodies before we get our crone schedules.

I did not know that life was so short when I started out. When I was in my twenties, it seemed to stretch endlessly out in front of me. Now, it feels as if it's been a matter of weeks, months, perhaps. Not more. The telescoping of the years when you look back on them is, to me, a peek at what things must look like to God, for whom there is no time. In a way, there's none for us either. Or at least, it is not as determinative of who we are as we once thought.

Here at Home

This afternoon, I am playing a CD on my new computer while answering email. All at the same time. Most of you know what an achievement this represents for me.

The music I have chosen is called *Notenbuchlein fur Anna Magdalena Bach*. She was *that* Mrs. Bach, married to Johann Sebastian, the Mrs. Bach of the 22 children. Her notebooks contain the music she and her children played when they were growing up—many lovely pieces by her famous husband, of course, but also things written by some of their gifted brood.

These pieces are small things. They have a domestic feel to them: one voice singing, or three or four, not a whole chorus. (Although the Bach kids would have outnumbered most Baroque choruses if they had all sung together!) A harpsichord all by itself, or with two mandolins. Music they played just for each other, to have fun and to learn.

How she found time, with 22 children, to make these notebooks is beyond me. I have never seen one, but several survive in museums: beautifully bound in leather and carefully written in her unmistakably 18th-century hand. I guess she knew that she was married to a genius, and how important it is to hold onto every scrap of what a genius produces. Or maybe not; maybe she was just a mom, and wanted something for her kids to do on rainy afternoons.

More than anything else, domestic life has made us what we are. We learn early how to fill the hours God gives us, and with what. We learn to be curious, or not to be. We learn that we can create, or we do not. Those who find themselves in charge of someone's formation for a season know how awesome a thing it is.

But it isn't only awesome. Mostly, domestic life is just fun. Mostly, kids learn by fooling around with interesting things. They stumble upon that which will enrich the world through their effort. We first learn to be who we are by playing.

This is also the way we first learn about love. Nobody sits us down and looks into our eyes and explains love to us. We soak it in casually and gradually, and it goes deep, like a long, light rain soaking into the ground. We learn first to need it and then to give it; finally, if all goes well, we learn to need to give it.

Joan and her sister were sitting with their dad. He was old and frail; they knew he was dying. They were fooling around, as they must have done many times when they were little: sitting on the floor, looking at old family pictures, identifying the people, laughing at the quaintness of them. Their dad lay on the couch nearby. He was too weak to talk or look at the old photos. They were playing, in a way, these grown women, and he was in the room with them, half-listening to their voices as he must have done a thousand times years ago. Half listening while he did something else years ago; it might have been reading the paper or paying bills. Now he was gathering himself to leave this world. It must have been lovely to leave that way, the last sounds in this world his children's voices talking and laughing quietly.

All the Bach children took their places among the dead centuries ago. Their voices have long since died away, their conversations, and the music their mom prepared for them in the notebooks. The parents must have loved listening to them play and sing. Maybe they sang while their parents lay dying, too, music to help them leave this world and enter the next. How lovely that would have been. A guitar plays a prelude I remember learning on the piano when I was little, an easy one, easy enough for a little girl to play.

I finish my email. It is as if they were here with me, those long-ago children of a famous father. It is as if we were keeping each other company, they with their music and I with my writing. It is as if we were all alive at the same time. And so we are, the living and the dead. Listen.

White Noise. Bright Noise.

At 4:30 a.m. the first one starts. One sleepy little chirp, and then a silence. He repeats, and then someone else answers from another tree. The birds are waking up. Soon the air is full of their music, each one with his or her own special song.

In the winter I am a radio addict—when I awaken too early, I want to listen to the news. But in the spring I leave the radio alone—the birds are entertainment enough.

At night it rains, and again I leave the radio alone. The sound of rain on the roof, against the windowpane, is one of humanity's safest sounds.

Outside, the cars on their way to the city begin to pass the house at about 5:30. *How can you stand the noise of the cars?* someone asks. *That's awful.* It isn't awful to me anymore. It's like the bird songs: one more species, going about its morning ritual. Off they go. Have a good day.

When we lived on West 12th Street, the ambulances used to scream their way past our building en route to St. Vincent's. When we moved over to West 11th Street, they screamed their way back, on their way out. Prayer for each run.

Late at night on 12th Street, the unmuffled sounds of the motorcycles would awaken us: Dykes on Bikes sometimes met there at midnight. Awful at first, but soon it was fine: Have a good ride, girls.

The sounds of the world swirling on and on around us are good sounds—even the unmuffled motorcycles. They are the sounds of a world in which I sit and watch and listen—they are not the sounds of a world of which I am in charge. I do not choose any of them; I don't start them or end them. They begin and fade away without me.

I turn on the computer and go to America Online. The guy says hello in a loud voice and I nearly jump out of my seat. He says I've got mail and I tell him not to yell at me. Some day I'll get used to him. In the meantime, he should stop yelling.

The Importance of Not Being God

Morning Prayer is most instructive these days—the lectionary readings are from Leviticus, and deal with how the worship of Israel, specifically how the doings of the priests—of whom Moses' brother Aaron is the prototype—are supposed to be conducted. Recently we read all about his ordination, which took seven days (ours only *seem* that long). It must have taken nearly seven days just to get them dressed, with all the ephods and blue robes with pomegranates on them which the priest seems to have been expected to make himself (no Wippell's catalogue, no altar guild)—and the checkered coat and a breastpiece (this is not like a bra, but more like a plate) and the Urim and Thummim that are supposed to sit in the breastpiece (so maybe it *is* a little like a bra). Aaron is also closely instructed about the construction of the holy space—where to put the ark, what kind of poles to suspend what kind of canopy and where—which, again, he appears to be expected to do himself.

I guess it has always been the case, then, that priests either create overblown expectations of themselves for themselves or have them created by the community. But lately, another voice has sounded: we're not supposed to run around like fools, doing everything ourselves. We're not supposed to get into such a state that all we communicate to the faithful is our own exhaustion. The kind of modeling we're supposed to offer is one of health and balance. I probably couldn't balance on a seesaw. I begin to question my vocation.

I read daily about the sex scandals in the Roman Church. I am aware of our own, and of those of virtually every faith community I know about. A class of people who are set apart for service easily comes to feel set apart by right, and easily becomes more interested in right than in service. That is the danger of any human authority. Special clothes, special chairs—a person can get to feeling pretty special.

And also, perhaps, put upon. I am struck by the fact that predators chose their victims in places where they are likely to be observed and apprehended: the Sunday school, among the choir, the acolytes. The organist, the church secretary—if it is an affair a clergyman wants, why does he focus on church people? Shouldn't he go outside, where he is less likely to get caught? But they rarely do. Makes me think an affair isn't really what's wanted at all. Maybe what's wanted is a kind of revenge.

Maybe it goes something like this: *I've given up so much. I make less money than other professionals. I don't have a family life because the church swallows all my time. I overwork and never get off the treadmill. I give so much.* Now I'm going to take something.

Sick? Yeah. But people who don't take care of themselves in good ways will take care of themselves in bad ways. Clergy need to come to terms with their own life choices and find good ways to live up to them. People need to understand that clergy are human with human needs, and then clergy need to let their people help them. For the most part, people will help, if they know the need. My recent experience with illness and burnout was, I think, typical: my people were most eager to help me slow down and work sensibly. It was I who could not let myself. I was *special*—my responsibilities were *special,* my call was *special,* my strength needed to be special, too. Probably everybody involved needs to tone down the *special* part.

Can appropriate self-care and moderation cure a pedophile of his disorder? I am sure it cannot—he needs to be isolated in such a way as to prevent him from hurting children. But might other, lesser disorders of the spirit and of the affections turn out differently if the self-image of clergy and the imaging of them by others were different? I bet they could. And, if even *some* of the heartbreak were to end with this generation, if even some of the future were to be different, it would be a great blessing.

Positive Stress Is Still Stress

Transplanting is hard on a plant. Even if it's from a ridiculously cramped, too-small pot to complete freedom to really spread out and grow in the ground, an unambiguously good move, the plant reels a little: the leaves droop, a flower may fall.

This is important for people, as for plants: positive stress is still stress. Even if a change is something you absolutely want very much, even if it's something of unquestionable good, change itself is stressful. Look at your own life: when you left home for the first time, full of excitement about your new life. Wasn't it stressful? I've known many people who showed the strain of that happy event: they lost or gained weight, got sick, felt depressed. I knew one young woman who began to obsess about dying when she went off to college. I know another who began to shoplift. Every new home, every new job, every new love—every new thing takes its toll. We mark the change by reeling a bit.

When I change, even when I change just a little, I also preside over the death of a portion of my old self. A part of me ceases to be, in order that a new part of me may live. The old me knew just what to expect. The new one isn't quite so sure.

We only reel for a little while. What gets a plant back on its feet is its roots: after a few days, they have twined and stretched and reached into the soil and discovered nourishment. The leaves and flowers display a new vigor, a hardy stiffness in the early morning breeze, a sturdy reaching toward the sun. The tough new roots now resist when you tug at the plant gently: *We ain't goin' nowhere,* they say silently. As soon as they sink into the ground and anchor there, they begin fighting the next change.

We are heartily orthodox creatures, plants and mortals. But we also tend inexorably to growth. We fight change and we insist upon it, all at the same time.

Where Is Jesus?

Today is the Feast of the Ascension, that odd observance of the simultaneous presence and absence of Jesus Christ. Up he goes, the risen Lord who has been with his friends for a remarkable set of weeks in which everything they thought they knew is turned upside down. I've always liked medieval depictions of the event: some of them have his feet sticking down out of a cloud, with all the people down below tilting their heads back and making identical Os with their mouths.

Well, the church had to think of something. "If Jesus was raised, where the heck is he?" newcomers must have asked. "Uh…up there," was the answer.

Up there. In the sky. Okay, I can see that. When the sun slants toward the earth in the early evening before it sets, so that its beams look something like a ladder or a path, I can imagine him coming to us on those beams. When the gentle rain falls on the garden, as it did last night, I can imagine him in each nourishing drop.

But he is also here. In the city, where the sunset is often barely perceptible because of the height of the buildings and the power of the neon lights, we look elsewhere for Christ. It would be a mistake for us to think he is not present in the teeming of it, in its immense drive and energy, both productive and misplaced energy: yeah, the boom box walking down the street and rattling your eardrums, the crowded sidewalk, the roar of the subway. All the power that humanity has harnessed, however we have harnessed it, for good or ill, would not be ours unless it were also his. In Christ, we say, we "live and move and have our being." *Being* is in Christ. *How* we will be is up to us.

Oh, please, you think as you read this, if I hear another damn boom box or another stupid car horn I'm going to go out there and throw an egg. My husband is a noise pollution vigilante: when we are on the street together he often terrifies me by scolding honking motorists vehemently, advancing toward them with a pointing finger and yelling. At such moments, with his wild hair, he looks like an anarchist from the 1930s, and I'm afraid he might annoy some meatball with a side arm who's having a bad day.

In my dream last night, the Eve of the Ascension, I was with several Roman Catholic women. We were at prayer together. I believe I was concerned about their not accepting me. We began the *Te Deum* in Latin, and I knew I would be found out: I could not get beyond the first line. I sensed that they knew this, that it was a test in some way. But I also sensed that it didn't really matter to them whether I knew the Latin or not, that the test was something like a little joke, a gentle teasing. I subsided into silence and listened as they repeated the ancient words. I wish I could report to you that I absorbed the Latin *Te Deum* perfectly in the night, but God saves miracles for more important stuff.

What mattered most was that it didn't matter that I didn't know. It didn't matter whether or not I was in the club. Jesus was now among us, everywhere. No matter where you live and no matter when. My husband Q, the sunlight streaming on the garden, the sauntering boom box, the car horns, the sweet rain, the birds awakening, the real anarchists from the 1930s, together with those whom they half scared to death, the Catholic ladies who knew Latin and liked me even if I didn't, Jesus the son of Mary and Joseph and somehow also the Son of God, all of us, the living and the dead, all in all, risen and rising, ascended and ascending. *Te Deum laudamus.*

Anyone Seen My Brain?

"What does Rosie think about it?" I ask Rosie.

My granddaughter looks at me and laughs. "I *am* Rosie, Mamo. You mean Madeline." They love it when I do this. Sometimes I run through the names of all my children and grandchildren before I hit upon the right one: "Corinna....uh, Anna....uh, Rosie.....uh, Madeline." I have even called Anna "Q" once or twice. I routinely confuse "breakfast" with "lunch," "radio" with "television." Someone will say "Gosh, that was great last night, wasn't it?" and I will have no idea what we experienced together the night before; it can take me ten or twenty seconds to find it in what's left of my brain. I forget whether or not I have taken my pills—I have to use one of those dumb compartmentalized pillboxes with the days of the week in large letters on them.

This is common enough to have a rueful name: it is called having a "senior moment." I remember that my father sometimes went through all our names before getting the right one too, and I remember thinking it was funny. I guess it still is. Even if it's me.

Actually, I don't see the harm in it. What does it matter if I get a name wrong? So what if I need a reminder about my medicine? I really, really love you....uh....well, you know who you are.

Another Chance

I did it again. It's been awhile, and I thought I was so much smarter. But no.

Sure, I said, *just let me know what you need.* It was my granddaughter's *Oklahoma* director. Costume crises. I've been there. I can sew. I usually come in at the eleventh hour for granddaughters' theatrical costume needs. No problem.

So I began Mother's Day with a couple of significant projects: shrink a women's size 10 jacket to fit an 86-pound seventh-grade boy. Add something to an old *Crucible* costume so it doesn't look 17th-century anymore. End of the19th is what we need for *Oklahoma.* Let's add that the *Crucible* costume is all black and very plain.

The jacket and the *Crucible* dress sat on the sofa all weekend. I didn't do anything on Mother's Day. The day after, one of the cats decided the *Crucible* dress was a latrine and acted accordingly. I discovered this today, after I had hauled the whole ensemble—jacket, dress, needle, thread—in on the train to New York, to work on between spiritual direction appointments at the convent on West 113th Street. I reduced the dimensions of the jacket uneventfully, but the dress was redolent of cat when I unfurled it to begin applying a froth of white lace to its plain black hem and sleeves. A sister dealt with it: all their winter habits were in the wash as they made the change from black to light blue for summer, so the convent laundry was a tidal wave of black serge anyway. One more black dress went along for the ride, with no one the wiser. It emerged after my 11:00 appointment, clean and sweet and waiting for its white lace ruffles. These were affixed on the train ride home, so the young lady who would wear the dress was not disappointed at 5 o'clock when rehearsal began.

What I wasn't going to do any more was wait until the last minute to begin enormous tasks. I was going to pace myself. I was going to be sensible.

But the delight of coming up with something beautiful just in time was just the same. The adrenaline of a performance: just the same. The satisfaction of making something out of almost nothing—a Beau Brummel's plumage out of a suburban matron's jacket, a prairie virgin's dance dress out of a Salem witch trial costume—is something I have never forgotten and would never want to lose. Some of us just love the thrill of the chase, the thinness of the ice. We want the stakes to be high enough and the odds against us great enough to make it...well, *interesting*.

Costuming these children was like costuming my own. Grandmothering them is like a second chance, a moment to do better what I think I might have done better years ago. Did I do it right? Was I a good enough mother? I sit and sew a lace ruffle on a 17th-century costume, and hope for the best the second time around. Probably I could have been a lot better, but I did the best I could. My own mother was already dead when my children were the age of these two girls, but I am alive. *My grandmother can sew that on for you,* says Madeline, when her friend loses a belt loop from her jeans. And I can, and I do, and I am so glad to be here still.

The Peaceable Kingdom

I understand there is such a thing as cat Prozac. I am in the market for some. Things are getting really rough, catwise, here on the Geranium Farm.

To begin with, Jenny died. She left this world on Christmas morning, and we buried her under the tree she used to love to climb. Jenny held on as long as she could—she was nineteen. That leaves Kate and What's-Her-Name. Kate is fifteen and What's-Her-Name is about two. Kate adopted Q at a beach house in 1987 and lived with him before we were married. They bought this house together. She opposed the match, and would not acknowledge my presence in the house for years. Couldn't understand why he needed to get married when he had her. When I came, with Jenny as my dowry, Kate turned up her nose at both of us.

What's-Her-Name joined us two years ago, using the name "April," a supernumerary cat from my daughter's house. She had already had an interesting life: she was found in a junkyard. This has left her with some odd habits: she jumps a mile when you make a sudden move anywhere near her, is afraid to go through a door if you're holding it open for her, and hides under things all day.

She and Kate cannot decide who is the alpha cat. The way they conduct the debate has me washing the living room and dining room curtains at least weekly and sometimes more often. The curtains are intended to pool gracefully on the floor in a fluid sweep of fabric, but the curtains are not the only things that pool in those rooms.

What's-Her-Name I can understand. She has no education. Kate, on the other hand, has spent her life in a genteel household with a well-mannered English professor as her closest friend. Neither of us ever squats down and pees on the floor while looking you right in the eye—ever—but that's what Kate has taken to doing. The night is shattered by her guttural howls at What's-Her-Name. She stands at the foot of the stairs and wails for Q to come and get her.

I wonder if the cat Prozac works. I bet it does. Imagine the peaceable kingdom we would inhabit if What's-Her-Name could just walk on by Kate without teasing her. If Kate could catch sight of her rival without pitching a fit. If I could go a week without washing the curtains. If we all could just get along.

I gather the newly sweetened curtains and put them in the dryer. We are like the cats, I think, unable to stop our escalating hostilities. We can't stop killing each other in the Middle East or anywhere else. We always have to have the last word, and so there is no last word. So we are animals, too, in the grip of negatives we can't seem to stop on our own. We can't seem to *get* the punishment we inflict upon ourselves, and so we go on and on inflicting more.

What cat Prozac would do, I understand, is enable Kate and What's-Her-Name to just walk on by. That would be a good thing. Good for them. Good for us. No last word. Just peace and quiet.

I Have Pain. I'm Not In Pain.

I thought it was my hip that had arthritis in it. Now my knee is getting into the act, too—lately, all the two of them ever do is complain. About the only time I feel all right is when I'm out walking. Then when I come home, they both let me have it. I'm up to *here* with their whining.

They are especially unhappy at night, it seems. Just when people are trying to sleep, they start in. I'm usually up with the two of them at about 3 a.m., and I don't want to wake Q up with my writhing. So I go into the India Room where I can writhe by myself.

You, perhaps, have not seen the India Room. It is our guest room, and it is furnished with things we brought back from India. And some other things that look like we brought them back from India. And some other things that don't look like that, but embrace the spirit of India, which is that everything is welcome and of value and probably beautiful in its way so we'd better keep it around just in case. So there is a detail from a Renoir print that I've had since childhood, and two wonderful photographs from an exhibit I once produced, and some bright saris over the top of the canopy frame, and some crystal paperweights, and a couple of candles, and some dried roses, and some beads from *mardi gras,* and two rugs that don't match at all, and some sandalwood beads, and a really cool plastic cross that Greg Johnson gave me and a sandalwood elephant whose tiny ivory trunk got broken and so Q replaced it with a piece of his own fingernail—honest. In the India Room, as in India itself, nothing is ever lost.

What's-Her-Name is usually in the India Room when I enter. She lies on the old Indian bedspread embroidered with mirrors and pearls. She spends hours there, adding to the riot with her calico-ness. Sometimes she seems to have turned on the radio to WNYE, where she likes to listen to the French broadcast. I'll go in there and turn it off and pretty soon it's on again. Why would an American cat want to listen to French radio? I slide in under the covers and writhe a little, trying to straighten myself out so my hip and knee will shut up already.

In India, there are many people around with terrible orthopedic conditions. They come from the brittle bones of malnutrition; it is also said that some of them are deliberately crippled in early childhood to make them compelling beggars. I don't know if that is so; India is so large and so complex that just about anything one could imagine is probably true—somewhere in it. Life is lived almost completely in public there; houses are not much at all, and many people don't have them—so you're outside, out in the clearing, out in the square, out alongside the road. The able-bodied and the disabled are side-by-side, all together. And people walk along on their elbows, on wheeled skate-board affairs because they have no legs, crawl along, walk painfully on one leg, beg vigorously with stumps of hands, intent on their task. I think of them as I sink into the wonderful mattress in the India Room. Of them on their mats, those who have mats. I think of the many who sleep on the bare ground. I think of their sore muscles and joints, of how they never improve. Of how alive they are anyway.

Pain isn't the last word. It's a thing you have—an unwelcome thing, to be sure, but not a thing that sums you up. You're more than your pain, more than your disability, more than the worst problem you have. The Frogs have finished their broadcast and the cricket scores begin. But I need not attend to them. I can sleep now.

Where the Cake Is

Today is the Feast of Pentecost. When I was little, I was often told it was the birthday of the church. *Where was the cake?* I wondered: I expected a birthday cake with candles, and such things were not part of church where I come from. The church's birthday seemed a rather ponderous affair, a state birthday—sort of like the birthday of the Queen Mother. Not a fun birthday like mine.

Later, when I was older and had been to more churches, I learned that it was also the celebration of the Holy Spirit's coming among us. I was informed of this in the 1960s, and this time there was no shortage of fun attached to the feast: flotillas of balloons released into the air to entangle themselves in jet engines and strangle innocent songbirds, clowns in the liturgy, liturgical dancers in the aisles, twenty-minute gospel readings in six different languages, parties afterward—with cake.

Today at Christ and St. Stephen's in Manhattan, as in many churches in the city today, two little babies were baptized. These were beautiful, with skin as soft as a feather. Neither one cried, although in my sermon I had given them both permission to do so. Instead, they regarded their own baptisms with grave interest, and allowed themselves to be anointed with chrism afterward with good grace. All the adults had soft smiles on their faces as they watched; for a moment, the compromises of our decades melted from us and we were pure and hopeful, like the two newest little Christians themselves.

The spirit gives the gift of life. Gave it at creation and gave it again at the first Pentecost. Gives it in the moment of forgiveness and in every sacrament of the church. Gives it at birth and continues to give it throughout life. Gives it at the moment of death and afterward, when we are all in Christ and Christ is all in all.

People Are Not Perfect

It was a familiar and unpleasant feeling: a tightness in my chest, matched by a tightness in my voice, my heart pounding hard enough for me to feel it. It's a feeling I used to have a lot and don't have much now. I was not happy to renew the acquaintance.

The person who occasioned it sat obliviously opposite me in our dining room. She was a houseguest neither of us had ever met, here to speak at a Compassionate Friends meeting and promote her recent book. Like us, she was a bereaved parent. Her daughter was killed in a car crash, smashed into a wall by a car that broadsided hers at 70 miles an hour. The 27-year-old—just married, beautiful, her mother's only child—died instantly. Her husband was terribly maimed. The driver left the scene on foot. The car was registered under a false name. No trace of him has ever been found, and it's been eight years.

Such a terrible story. Such heartbreak. And there I sat, listening. And who made my heart pound with anger?

It was the mother. The bereaved mother. She was talking about how the man who killed her daughter was an illegal alien—she concluded this, although he had never been found, on the basis of an eyewitness statement that he appeared to be Mexican. She was recently excused from jury duty, she said, because the defendant was an illegal alien. "So you generalize from this experience to all illegal aliens?" I asked. *Well, yes*, she answered, as if her answer were obvious, the only possible one, and went on to describe how likely illegal aliens are to be lawbreakers, to be drug runners, to be criminals.

She went on. Her daughter's new in-laws had their hands full caring for their son. She had visited a few times, and then they had cut her off from visiting her son-in-law. It hurt her. She loved her daughter's husband, and he connected her with her daughter in a way she needed and wanted. Who could not understand that? But she continued to explain with bitter what-do-you-expect resignation that, after all, they were *English*, and that everybody knew what *they* were like. The coldness of the in-laws was because they were English.

I am so sorry her daughter has died. I am so sorry she must rebuild her life alone. I wish with all my heart it had not happened. But, most of all, I am sorry that her response to this tragedy has been to use it to fuel a view of the world that divides people into groups and judges them accordingly. All undocumented people didn't kill her daughter. *One* did. All English people didn't cut off contact with her; *one* family did. My father was English, and he would never have treated anyone that way.

What *is* it in us that responds to terrible things by making the world more terrible, to cruelty by being cruel, to the slaughter of the innocent by including other innocents in our revenge? The World Trade Center is now a thirty-foot steel pillar and a few piles of rubble in a hole in the ground because of people who acted in hatred of a group. When will we ever learn?

I lay in bed when the house was asleep, unable to sleep because I was so angry at her. I'm going to tell her, I told my husband. I'm never going to see her again, and I'm just going to tell her that she's being unfair in a way that is no tribute to her daughter's memory, in a way that excuses and causes more violence. Just because you have suffered is no reason to make other people pay for your suffering, people who have done nothing to cause it. Just because you have suffered doesn't mean that henceforth you'll never have to examine your own actions, statements and motives. Just because you're a tragic figure doesn't mean you are not still a moral agent.

The next morning was a lovely one, soft sun and sweet air. Birds were at the feeder, and other birds sang in the trees. The warring cats were in a cease-fire, each at her bowl of food, focused on the business at hand. My tea was ready. Our guest came down, and Q made her some toast. We sat at the table. I had a candle lit; we often have breakfast by candlelight.

I never delivered my little sermon on tolerance. I listened to her talk about her daughter. I thought as I listened that this was a limited person who had had a terrible thing happen to her, and that she was not likely to hear me if I lectured her. This was a guest in my home. I would be hospitable.

Now she is gone, and I will never see her again. She was good at the Compassionate Friends meeting, a good listener to the other bereaved parents.

My pounding heart subsided. People are limited. They are not perfect. They have prejudices of which they are unaware, and the process of awareness is just that: a process.

Get Wisdom

Some days, from 10 a.m. to nearly noon, Rosie and I go to the library. We sit at the same table every time. She does schoolwork. I read back issues of *Christian Century* and magazine articles about John Walker Lindh for an upcoming book. Oh, all *right*—sometimes I also read catalogues.

My first library was in a recycled Methodist church. It was tiny. My mother or father took me every Saturday afternoon. Children's books were at the back, and there were little stools you could sit on while you looked at books. I was allowed to take out three, and exchanged them the next week for another three. When I was seven, I decided it was time for me to read more serious books than the picture ones I had favored earlier. I checked out a thick book called *A Child's History of the World*—the world seemed a good place to start becoming an educated person. *A Child's History of the World* was several hundred pages long, a hefty read for a seven-year-old. As the week drew to its close, I knew I would not finish it by Saturday. Don't worry, my mother said, you can renew a book. The amused librarian renewed my obsession several times that summer, as I read about ancient Egypt and Greece and Rome and medieval cathedrals and worked my way forward to the American Revolution, where the book stopped. I seem to remember that "the world" had a distinctly Western slant. But it was a beginning.

A library has a certain feel to it. It is quiet. It is full of quiet people, people finding things out. It is filled with the smell of books, of old paper and old glue and leather. Pages turn, a newspaper rattles, the librarian really does *Sssh!* you if you do more than whisper.

There are several libraries at Rutgers. The one in which I most loved to work was the library of the New Brunswick Theological

Seminary, which is a hundred years old and beautifully paneled and balconied inside. It has a statue of Hagar and Ishmael in a prominent place—interesting choice. My favorite art in the library was a mosaic memorial plaque about a deceased Dutch Reformed clergyman, showing the worthy man's broad face and flowing white hair and black hat and the words: *After his sermon, on the Lord's Day, God took him.* And he'll take you, too, seemed the implicit message, if your sermons go on too long. To this day, I never go beyond twelve or thirteen minutes. Just in case.

The heavy 19th-century books about ancient Christian writers of the patristic period were my massive companions in those days. They didn't circulate; you used them there. It seems now that time stood still while I read them and made notes on cards about them.

The library at General Seminary faces Ninth Avenue. The traffic noise barely invaded the quiet, though; once in a while, a horn or a siren would break into the silence, but ordinarily just the familiar hush and occasional footfall, the rare whispered conversation. My carrel was home; I could go immediately to it if I were to walk in there today, twenty-five years later. I wonder who is sitting there now, in my chair. The feel of the wood, the pressure of that particular chair on my particular back, all those things conditioned me to readiness to learn.

That's the deal for Rosie. The same place every day. The same chair. The same hush, punctuated these days by the quiet tapping of computer keys. Your senses can help you *learn* to *learn*, if you train them right. You can learn to love quiet, even if it's only for a short time. Places can teach us, can help us reach further into our minds than we usually go and find treasures there we didn't know we had.

Get wisdom, the writer of Proverbs barked recently in one of the Daily Office readings, *and whatever else you get, get insight.* This sounds a little like wisdom is something you could pick up at the store—*Got wisdom?*—but he doesn't mean that. Acquire it. Find it and savor it. Learn to learn it. Condition yourself to receive it. Stop for awhile and go to a place where you can learn to learn.

Memorial Day

The colonial cemetery in our town sits on a hill next to the train station, as it did not in the 18th century. Old cemeteries are ordinarily on hills—not just because of the sacred proximity to the sky and to heaven, but because the risk of contamination is high in low-lying areas. The old stones lean against each other after more than 200 years in the ground. Many have toppled and lie, flat and exhausted, against the grassy ground. One of them has grown right into the side of an enormous tree.

Different stones were used by different generations of stonecutters. Some of the oldest have fared the best, and their death's-head angels stare clearly back at you, with their limerick-like warning:

Take heed, all you who pass me by:
As you are now, so once was I
As I am now, so you shall be,
So be prepared to follow me.

Others are barely legible, just a letter here and there, a number, a blurred unidentifiable image. The 19th century applied weeping willows to the stones, and original, more ethereal poems about the joys of heaven. The stones give the ages, not just in years but in months and days: whoever says people in former times took death more easily because it was more frequently experienced in everyday life hasn't spent much time in cemeteries, where the stones attest to the struggle of the living to find comfort in honoring so minutely the days of the lives of the dead.

Our eleven Revolutionary War soldiers each have a special medallion and a special little flag. Confederate soldiers were buried where they fell, elsewhere. Elderly wives lie next to husbands who preceded them into the next world by many decades, and the graves of children are everywhere.

Many of you remember when Memorial Day wasn't just about the war dead, but about all the dead. When a trip to the cemetery was a part of the day, to pull away weeds, to plant flowers and cut the grass. With the medicalization of death has come a similar distancing of the living from the dead: they no longer guide us with their silent presence among us. Now, they just disappear.

At St. Clement's, the new columbarium has about seven residents. I often used to see someone visiting the dead there, standing next to the wall of niches with a hand on one special one, or sitting in a chair and spending time together. Sometimes I would find a flower in a vase. How nice, I would think, to be able to stay in proximity. We know each other primarily by means of our physical bodies in this life. To continue to want proximity implies no disrespect to the world of the spirit in which they now live. "Disrespect" is probably not a thing about which the dead worry overmuch; that concern is ours, not theirs.

I don't care what you do with me, someone will say. *I won't really be there.* Well, yes and no. The dead are in Christ, and Christ is all in all. All in the spirit, in the mysterious existence the living cannot yet understand, and all in the hearts of the bereaved, with their concrete memories and physical, specific grief.

Monday there will be a parade in our town. It starts at the Memorial Park and goes down Main Street. The high school band and flags march in it, as do the police and firefighters with their shiny fire engines and the DAR and the American Legion and the Veterans of Foreign Wars. It goes right by the colonial cemetery, where the dead lie, silent in what remains of their coffins, inadequately named by their illegible, crooked stones. The new cemetery is on the other side of town, orderly and level, with paved drives and careful plantings. You will not be able to hear the high school band from there: it is too far away.

Guard Against Infection

We swam in the creek every summer. Waded, really—Deer Creek was too shallow in most places for swimming. But you could stand on rocks and put your feet in, or ride inner tubes down the lazy stream, or swing from a rope and let yourself fall into a slightly deeper part here and there. However hot it was, it was always cool by the creek. Grownups could sit on the creek bank and talk, knowing that there wasn't much in the way of trouble to be gotten into, even for the most enterprising child.

But this particular summer, nobody was in the creek. Nobody's parents would let them go—there was polio in it, everybody said, you would get polio if you went in the water. We all lined up for injections; I indulged in high drama, complete with real tears, about getting a needle, but it was no use—everybody had to get one. A couple of years later the Sabin oral vaccine was released for public health use, and children everywhere breathed a sigh of relief. One less terror.

I don't know if there really was polio virus in Deer Creek. But today I received an email that purported to be *from* me—now that was different. I had gotten one purporting to be from another friend but suspiciously named "Honey"—*hmmnn.* Maybe she was sending me a joke? I got another one that wanted to tell me something about "cell-spacing," whatever that is, from another friend to whom I had just been speaking online and he hadn't mentioned anything about cell spacing. *Hmmmn* again.

The polio in the creek, whether it was really there or not, was not there because of the deliberate action of anybody. The viruses that people inadvertently circulate on computers *are*—a concept that baffles me completely. Who has a life empty enough to play malicious tricks on strangers? And why?

The cheerful anarchy of the Internet is built upon a trust that Christian theology knows enough to view with suspicion—you don't have to be too strong a believer in original sin to know that the very presence of the opportunity to do mischief is enough to at least plant the idea in our minds. Bob Herbert of the *New York Times* talked today about the dissonance between human beings' sincerely held longing for peace and our almost-universal insistence on war. We may want to share and treat one another well, but we seem also to want to dominate and intimidate. We seem to do both at the same time. The polio virus, killer though it was, was not in it to dominate. It was just trying to survive. The creator of the computer virus can make no such claim—he's animated by plain meanness.

I read the psalms every morning and every evening. For many years, I and many people I know have been embarrassed by some of them—the ones asking God to do horrible things to the enemy, the ones describing in graphic detail just what kinds of physical tortures the enemy should undergo. Some of our lectionaries are too civilized even to include those harangues in public worship—they omit the nasty verses, put them in parentheses so you'll know to skip them.

I don't skip them, though, embarrassing as they are. It's pretty important to understand how close violence is to us in our tradition. It's important, especially, for us not to think that it is *other* cultures and *other* religions that are tempted by it, while we have always been people of peace. Not *always*—read the psalms.

What did the Unabomber want? He wanted a world in which people were free and humane, in which machines didn't alienate people from one another and from the fruit of their labor. Those are good things. And what did he do to bring them about? You remember.

You need to run an anti-virus scan through your computer today. You need to be careful about opening emails from people you don't know, or even from people you do know if the subject line seems odd. If you're a creative type, you may need to go easy on the eye-catching subject lines for a while, if you want people to read your stuff. You need to protect yourself. This may mean you are inconvenienced a bit while you check on the authenticity of a message. What a pain.

That whole summer we couldn't swim. What a pain—it was hot. We nagged our parents, but it was no use. We all went back to the creek the next summer, with our inoculations up to date and the polio epidemic already slipping into history. It was safe now.

It's Never Really Over

I remember thinking, often, that the site of the World Trade Center would just never be cleaned up. There's too much here, I would think as I looked at the immense pile. They'll never get it all. I did imagine an empty lot with one sole remaining brick sitting in it. Of course, there really weren't bricks there. That, too, was an imagining.

And now, they've got it all. They cut the last column down this morning. They draped the poor thing in a flag, just as if it were a person. Right up until the end, they were finding remains, each one an astonishment at this late date. But now they will find no more there. They've found what they're going to find. Maybe there will be something over in the landfill now and then, but this is basically it.

They never found Glen Miller. They never found Michael Rockefeller. They never found Amelia Earhart. Come to think of it, they never found Jimmy Hoffa and they never found Adolph Hitler. The good and the bad have death in common; it comes to everyone. And when they are not found, so that we can mark their death, something strange happens: they seem to live. We can't seem to close the book on them. Maybe Hitler's in Australia or Argentina, people still say, although he'd be over a hundred years old if he were. Maybe Jimmy Hoffa made it out of the Meadowlands alive. Maybe Amelia Earhart lived, maybe Michael Rockefeller went native. Maybe they're all still alive, an irrational piece of us says, even though we know the truth. They're not still alive. They died.

Thousands of people walked and crawled and were carried out of the World Trade Center. More than thirty thousand, some say. We would marvel at the fact that almost everybody lived if we weren't still so heartbroken over those who died. We know how hard everybody tried—even the buildings stood as long as they could, and then one groaned and sank, layer upon layer. Then the other. Three thousand of the thousands didn't make it out. We have about a thousand of them. The rest went to dust as quickly as their souls went to heaven.

And we are still here. Peoples' lives are still frayed in many places, and none will ever be as before. Life is never *as before.*

What would have formed us in these months, if this tragedy had not? Something else. Gary Condit, maybe. Some young rock singer's rehab experience. Enron, of course. We would be just as puzzled and angered by the situation in the Middle East as we are now. Argentina would still have gone bankrupt. Somebody would have noticed that people are now buying $10,000 television sets and wondered what could make one worth that amount of money.

We would have half-focused on a lot of different things. We would have continued our 500-channels-but-nothing's-on lives. For a season, we all paid attention. Something gripped us all, and it was something worth being gripped by.

Maybe what happened was that we grew up a bit. It is children who are easily distracted and pay attention to small matters. Adults do adult things. This was a very adult thing. Even the children joined in, standing in awe of something much bigger than they were, drawing pictures of it, writing letters. We stood united, if only for a while. Or maybe for longer. It is, after all, completely up to us what kind of people we will be.

How Do You Know God Loves You?

How do you know God loves you? How do you know God even exists?

I don't think there is any question I have been asked more often, with more urgency, than this basic one. Idle curiosity *never* prompts it. It is asked urgently, or not at all. So:

I anthropomorphize our cats. To a scandalous degree, imputing to them all manner of human emotions and motivations they cannot possibly possess: I think Kate's in love with my husband, think the late, lamented Jenny viewed herself as a nurse, think What's-Her-Name is fired with ambition to be taller than she is. I think I have a relationship with the cats, an emotional one, and I think that it is somehow reciprocal—even though anyone who watched them stare into the middle distance without a sound for hours on end when we are together in the same room, might reasonably conclude that they're really not holding up their end.

They provide little evidence of emotional involvement with us. But we believe in it. This belief is part of who we are. It is one of our favorite things, making up stories about the cats and their inner lives.

With my husband, the evidence is stronger. I think he loves me. Know it, even. I base this belief on his behavior. He listens to me and talks to me. He compliments my cooking and cooks for me. He shares everything he has with me. He edits my writing. He worries about my health. He likes my back rubs, and he rubs my sore knee and makes it feel better. He is interested in my past, even when I am reticent about it. He tells me I am beautiful, even when that's not really the truth. So I have evidence that he loves me.

But sometimes he does not do these things. Sometimes we have an argument. Sometimes he is not at home. Sometimes I am angry at him. Sometimes the evidence fails.

But I still know he loves me, even when the evidence is not there. Knowing he loves me is part of who I am now. This belief helps constitute me. I am made of it. I would not be myself if I did not believe it. It is conceivable that it is not so, that I am mistaken, that he doesn't love me at all. I know a woman who thought her husband loved her very much, until one day he told her that he had a whole other family, a common-law wife and a child, and that he wanted to leave her and live with them. Oh.

Such things have happened. They are conceivable. So the woman had to reconstitute herself. She had to be remade, because part of what made her was her knowledge of her husband's love. If such a thing were to happen to me, I would have to be remade, too. But I am constituted, in part, by my faith in Q. I am me because he is himself.

And God? The same. The evidence is sometimes there for us and sometimes it is not. We look at the Grand Canyon and say that God is mighty and good. We look at the bubonic plague and we are not so sure. My life has had great joy and great sorrow—I could not begin to compare relative amounts of either, but it has had its share of both. I believe in God. I believe in the love of God. It is part of who I am to believe. If I did not believe, I would have to be reconstituted. I am me because God is God.

There is not some secret body of knowledge I have that makes me believe. I don't know anything nonbelievers don't know. I have no new evidence. I look at the same world they see, the same mixture of pain and delight, of beauty and ugliness, the same blend of kindness and cruelty they see. Just the same, though different every day. We all see the same thing.

But I have become a person who is constituted by her belief. I believe when there is ample evidence, and I believe when there is none. Faith is not a matter of evidence. It is, I think, a matter of self. *Credo, ergo sum:* I believe, therefore I am.

In the Garden

There are adult sites on the Internet, you know. Once in a while, I get an email inviting me to look at one. You can tell because the word "hot" is usually in the title somewhere. When I first got my computer, I was incensed at receiving the invitations: I thought they were targeting me directly and had misunderstood me profoundly. I thought I was about to be buried under a grimy avalanche of unsolicited porn. But now I know that everyone gets these, and that all you have to do is delete them. You don't have to write AOL a frantic email, like I did. AOL wrote back kindly, saying they were sorry I had received it and to contact them if I had further problems. *Get a life*, they probably thought as they pressed "Send," but they betrayed no such impatience.

I do have my vices. The White Flower Farm catalogue is one—it is on my favorites list and I binge on it often. They tempt me with their descriptions: Will I go to the blues and violets right away, or will I look first to see what's on sale? Lilies? New Irises? More lavender? Soon the bulbs for fall planting will appear—I visit every day to see if they've arrived. Will I lust after birdbaths? *Ooh—a copper one!* Will I buy things without telling my husband? I have a modest criminal record in this area, and am striving for more transparency.

Mostly, I don't buy. I just look. We would have to buy more property if I bought everything I wanted, and there is no more property on either side of us. Yesterday, though, I couldn't resist. I came across a flower named "Viola Victoria Cawthorne." Cawthorne! Not such a common name. And Victoria Cawthorne! I have a cousin named Vicky—that's got to be her. My cousin has a violet named after her.

Our fathers came from England just after the First World War, with the rest of their family. They were alike in many ways: handsome and scholarly, men of few words. Men who loved history and loved to read about it. Men who sometimes seemed not to be at home in the world as it was. And they both loved gardens and flowers. My dad's garden was bountiful and beautiful. He and I, being early risers, would go out in it every morning. He'd poke around with his hoe, stoop to pull a weed. Little was said, and nothing needed to be said. The silence was fine with me. To this day, I am quickly exhausted by chatter.

Then we would go inside for breakfast. He would make us tea and toast and we would sit at the kitchen table. He would read his prayer book and then his seed catalogue. This, too, was largely a silent time. Then he would go to work.

Decades later, this is still the kind of morning I like. I usually put the tea on first and then step outside for a quick tour to see how everyone is. The trumpet vine, after feigning death well into May, burst one night into full leaf and within a couple of weeks had destroyed one of the back steps by sending out a tendril to grow right up through it. He has also invaded the peonies again, and reaches aggressively toward the shingles on the house itself, getting closer every day. He's been too busy with his imperial ambitions even to think about producing any flowers, but Old Trumpet is a quick study: he'll remember his duty and make them overnight at the last minute. His flowers are great fun: they have a pocket of air at the bottom of their horn-shaped blossoms, which you can pop in just the same way you can pop that bubble wrap that comes in packages. I look forward to it every year. Old Trumpet is also a magnet for hummingbirds, Q tells me, and he has seen them. I have not seen the hummers, because I've not been home much during the day before, but I will be lying in wait for them this year.

I must find my cousin and find out if she is the Victoria Cawthorne of flower fame. I know it is she. I know it. And I bought three of her violets. I can't wait to see what they look like.

Come to Mama

Today I began my campaign to lure a hummingbird to our garden in 2002.

Here is what is in place and what is planned: bright red or orange or purple flowers with tubular shapes. The hummers have long thin beaks, through which they sip nectar out of tubular flowers. They like bright colors, reds and purples. Today I planted some reds—they're not exactly tubular, but they're red, and the book says you can trick a hummer into visiting you just by tying a red ribbon to a plant so he thinks it's a red flower. Then he comes to see what it is and you've got him. So a red flower should certainly do it get one on the property, even if it isn't his favorite.

Of course, once you've brought him in, you do have to have something to offer. He's not going to be satisfied with a red ribbon. So I'm going to the bird place to find hummingbird feeders, into which you put sugar water. You can dab some red nail polish on them, it says—I am beginning to think the hummers really aren't very smart.

Once they get sugar water and sweet bright tubular flowers, the book promises, they're yours. I can't wait. I want to see them. They expend so much energy they eat many times their weight in food every day—something else we have in common.

The hummers make me think about churches and their desire to have new people join them. It's one thing to get them in the door, but you have to have something to give them once they're there. It has to be something you know they'll love, and you know this by asking yourself what you love. And then by asking others what they love. And then—the hardest part—by respecting the fact that everyone doesn't love the same thing. That churches can do more than just one thing. More than just one way.

The book says that not every hummingbird feeder will work. It says that the hummers aren't drawn to the feeders that appeal most to human good taste—elegant glass ones with sleek spouts, expensive trimmings, Tuscan-looking ceramic ones. We may like them, but we're not trying to attract *ourselves*. We're already here. We're trying to attract hummers. The book says the feeder I want looks like a pie plate with a red lid. Probably not something I would choose.

Lots of times churches tell themselves they want lots of different kinds of people in their congregation, but present only things that will appeal to those who are already there. They want young people, but with the musical tastes of 50-year-olds. International people, but with American tastes. Gay people who look straight. Women who think like men. Poor people, but with money.

The folks who are already around react with suspicion and even hostility to new things. *We don't do things this way. It's just not* us. But isn't that just the point? It's *not* us. It's us plus *others,* and us plus others *won't* be just like *us* was. If I want a hummingbird to visit me, I won't get him with sunflower seeds and peanuts. With those, I will get the wonderful birds I already have. I'll keep putting out the sunflower seeds for them, but if I want the hummer, I must also put out what he eats. And hope he sees the red flowers. And comes closer to take a look.

An Uninvited Guest

Uuugghh.

Hard to think, when you happen to be the host, that all a virus is trying to do is the same thing we're all trying to do: find a place to live and a job and keep food on the table. At first I thought it was something simple, like congestive heart failure—heart patients jump quickly to conclusions—but it's a bug. The same bug that is devouring many New Yorkers: congested chest, fatigue, painful sinuses. Aches and pains, I hear, although how would I know, with all the aches and pains I already have?

It was Jane Austen who wrote, as if offhandedly, "My headaches are so much worse than other people's. Jane Austen was *never* offhanded. She caught, in that terse line, the voluptuous extravagance of self-pity that engulfs the most sober among us when we don't feel well. We feel as if it is not just an inconvenience, but an outrage.

It isn't, of course, it's just a virus trying to find an apartment. I may feel it doesn't belong inside me, but it feels right at home. *Nice place*, it says, looking around at the *ciliae* lining my bronchial tubes. *Maybe I'll stay another week.*

All manner of living things make themselves right at home in places where they weren't before, always to the annoyance of the host. Sparrows and starlings are not native to North America, for example, although they are probably now our most common birds. They were brought here by some educated fool who wanted North America to have all the birds mentioned in Shakespeare. Oh, *that's* a good idea.

Kudzu was brought from Japan to the American south, where it was thought it would make a lovely ground cover because it grew so fast. You bet it does. Dixie is carpeted with the stuff today, and the weekend warriors are out there every Saturday doing battle with it. *The timeless beauty of natural bamboo,* an ad in a nursery catalogue said. Q saw it and smiled grimly: he spends hours chasing down *punghi* stakes that spring up overnight, to a height of a foot or two, six or seven every night. The timeless beauty has traversed an entire driveway and half a yard, underground, to spring up on the other side in the midst of the hedge. Q treats it with something resembling napalm; he always feels a little soiled after his chemical warfare against the bamboo. It's not from here. It feels like an outrage. But the bamboo doesn't know about outrage. *Nice place,* it says to itself, *wonder what's over there behind the garage?*

There are things we just have to accept. Bamboo may not be from here, but it's here now, and we have to deal with it. Sparrows. Starlings. I may be an outraged host to my awful virus, but I'm still a host, and I have to deal. There wasn't a special arrangement made about me with a provision that I would never get sick. That I alone would proceed along the road of life with only my own ideas and plans informing it. Foreign stuff comes into life. Changes you didn't author happen to you. All the time. Nobody gets to stand beside the piano and sing "I Did It My Way," except Frank Sinatra. And he died, too. Not every thing was his way, I guess.

So get over it. I'm not special. Stuff happens. Happens to me. Be over eventually. Going to have some hot tea now.

Change Something

It's important to have a beautiful office. At St. Clement's, I had a beautiful office: gorgeous dark woodwork, lovely wine-red walls, track lighting, stained glass windows.

Here my office is a work in progress. The walls are pale lemon yellow. It occurred to me recently that, this being the case, I could theme the office to match the national flag of Sweden. My mother was Swedish. My father was English, and somehow I didn't think I'd get much work done in a red, white and blue office. But blue and yellow. Sun, sea and sky. Flower blue. Creamy lemon yellow. Yum.

Besides, the recliner chair was looking elderly. Years of kicking back had done their worst, and it needed an upholstery job. So I could change colors: I could do the chair in blue.

Upholstering a reclining wing chair proved too pricey for someone with no job to contemplate. Slipcovers, then: the world is currently awash in cool one-size-fits-all slipcovers. I looked, I shopped, I bought: a medium blue with white flowers.

One size fits almost all. The chair is substantial: you can buy one-size fits-all slipcovers for recliners, but recliner wing chairs are a breed unto themselves. Trying to install the medium blue with flowers reminded me of my grandmother getting into her girdle. Eventually, I gave up. No medium blue with flowers.

Then I found it: blue check, for a wing chair. I measured this time—slow learner—and it came. And it fit. Of course, the chair no longer reclines, but this is an *office*. I also got some more blue check fabric to do a window treatment.

The room is small. What do you think, I ask Q. He looks at the blue-checked window and the blue-checked large chair in the small room. *You know that ad for Target—"Change something," with the Swedish lady in red checks in a red checked kitchen and red checked towels and a red geranium? It looks like that.*

So much for spousal loyalty. Wait until he wants to know what I really think of his homemade falafel. I go back in the office for another look. He's right, damn it. Too much large blue check in too small a space. The room looks nervous, and a little desperate, more like a going-out-of-business Mom and Pop restaurant than like the calm of sun and sky. The art on the walls looks funny now, too.

Something else at the window, I guess. Something light and airy, like clouds in the sun and sky in stupid damn Sweden, where the sun doesn't even know enough to go down at night at certain times of the year.

But I am coming to love my Change Something office anyhow, even if I do need to redo the window. I love hearing birds out the window—and passing cars, too. I can tell the time by the traffic volume. I love my computer—imagine. I love my comfortable desk chair. I love the way the artwork that hung on the walls of my office at St. Clement's mixes with what was already here. I love my new phone that cost $29, even if I can't make the handset work. I mostly don't want to talk to anybody anyhow—isn't that why God made email?

Do you miss it? people are always asking. *Yes*, I answer, always, but each time a little voice inside me reminds me that I like my new life. That I love it, even. Life and time go on, and we go on with them. Nothing stays the same. We can fight it, but we won't win. Best to just jump in the river of life and see where it takes us. Probably somewhere good.

Better Living Through Chemistry

Kate the tortoiseshell cat and I have the same thing: arthritis in the hip. I also have it in one knee. Kate doesn't have knees.

I obtained a famous arthritis drug and began taking it. It helped. Then I read an article that said the report exonerating it from doing unspeakable things to one's stomach may have been...well, overstated. Damn. Then a friend told me about an herbal concoction that worked wonders for her. And her husband. Helps your body make more cartilage to stick between your creaky bones. Well okay; I want more cartilage. It's expensive, she warned; twenty dollars a bottle. Since the famous pharmaceutical ran $140.00, this looked like a bargain. Take three a day for a month, said the lady at the health food store. Then maybe two a day. Give it some time. Okay.

Kate had begun emitting a strange cry, a deep, from-the-gut wail. She uses it to summon Q to make her breakfast—I am convinced that she is crying *wolf* in the morning, just to get him out of bed—but she also wailed, sometimes, lying right in her chair. Then she was definitely not crying *wolf*. It was not a happy sound. It sounded like pain to me. Arthritis in the hip, the vet said, and gave us a pill that looks suspiciously like the one I am taking. Kate weights 7 pounds; she only needs one a day. She's stopped wailing, except for her breakfast. I think we're both feeling better.

She hates her pill. Q and I both got punctured when we tried a two-person approach, I at her mouth and he pinning all four limbs. She did get the pill down. He tried putting it in her food, but she just turned up her nose and let What's-her-Name have it all. I have had some good luck with crushing it, combining it with softened butter and anointing her paws with it—she then, being a cat, cleans her paws and eats the medicine. We'll try that again this morning.

She doesn't want her pills. I don't want mine, either, and I take a lot more than Kate—nine a day, I think, which seems like an awful lot. It was not long ago that I took no medicine at all. How simple and sweet that was—I didn't appreciate it. Odd, that I feel reluctant about the medicine, since it keeps me alive and functioning. Nobody is holding me down and shoving it down my throat, as we were doing with Kate, or smearing me with butter and demanding that I lick it off, as we are doing now. But I count out the pills and toss them back, and I feel a little put upon each time I do, as if doing so were somehow difficult. It really isn't.

We attach an inappropriate moral freight to medicine, as if it were sinful, somehow, to take medicine instead of doing without it. This is less true of my heart medicine, but it's really strong where my antidepressant medicine is concerned: wouldn't a good person just be able to give herself a shake and get over it? Shouldn't I be able to do this "by myself?" I ask the psychiatrist how long I'll be on this stuff. He suggests that it's really too soon to ask. Do you want to be off it? *Well,* I say, *it seems like I should. I don't like taking the pills.* As if it's hard to take them. And it's not.

Do I feel better because of the medicine? Absolutely. Am I more useful because of it? Oh, yeah. I don't cry every five minutes, or tremble with anger. I can make decisions based more on what makes sense rather than on a neurotic sense of martyred duty. I feel entitled to self-care, rather than perversely proud of doing without it. All these are good things.

And do all these good things come out of a bottle of pills? No, they come out of my own mind and spirit. They were blocked from their graciousness by chemicals, and chemicals have restored them to it.

They do not make me into someone else. They make me more who I really am.

So does the arthritis potion, I guess. Maybe who I really am is a skinny dancer who can put her legs behind her head. I would be one of few grandmothers who could do that. And the skinny part would be a first. We'll see.

Sweet Dreams

The ancients, of course, believed that God spoke to them in dreams. Joseph and his dreams of stardom—always liked that guy. The insecure, powerful king consulting visionary Daniel and hearing not-so-great news. The other Joseph, Jesus' father, and his dreams of warning. Pilate's worried wife, trying in vain to prevent the crucifixion. Peter and his vision on the rooftop telling him to lighten up already about demanding kosher observance of new Christians.

I actually think God speaks to us in dreams, too, even today. They are powerful narratives in which the rules don't apply, at least not in the normal way: in dreams, the dead live again, we know things without being told, we show forth our secrets and our greatest fears in symbolic actions and situations. I know a young woman preparing for graduate school: she dreams she's at her old high school, can't find her classes, doesn't know where to go, wakes up in a cold sweat. Guess she's worried, in some part of her spirit, about such a big step into the future. Decades after my own graduation, I still have dreams in which I am registered for a math class, haven't done any of the work and am now about to take the final. Let me just say that the young woman with the dream and I are closely related—oh, all right, it's Anna. And that Corinna has had these dreams, too. And let me just say that my mother had such dreams of academic unpreparedness until the end of her life.

In other dreams, it is not hidden worry but magical power that shows itself as part of us. I often dream I can fly: I approach an obstacle, falter a bit, and then remember my power. I don't have to be stopped by this: I can fly right over it. I stretch out my arms and up I go. The obstacle looms dangerously in front of me, but I remember that height is no problem, that flying high is no harder than flying low, and I clear the hurdle by a long shot. Another young woman tells me of a flying dream she had: with her was a little girl, and she showed the child how to fly high above the trees. *I think the little girl was me, too,* she said, and I nodded. Both her adult self and her childhood self could fly. Old limitations and weaknesses did not apply. It was a joyful dream.

And another: a young woman whose father abandoned her as a child now has a very guarded relationship with him. She does not speak freely to him—she doesn't know what the market will bear in this relationship, how far to trust it. She dare not risk angering him—what if he disappears again? But in her dream, she strides into his living room and confronts him as he sits in his chair. She denounces him like an Old Testament prophet, points her finger, shouting her truth to him in majestic, wrathful cadence, over and over. This anger is righteous. She awakens having told a truth. She may never be able to speak with utter freedom to him in the flesh, but she has done it in her dream. And she has increased her own righteous power.

What does God want you to know? That the life containing and surrounding this one is good. That your fears are real and deserve a hearing. That you have more power than you think you have. That those you have loved and lost, love you still.

"I never remember my dreams," someone tells me. "I want to have a dream in which my mom comes back from being dead and tells me she's all right. But I never remember my dreams. I don't think I *do* dream."

Everyone dreams. Every dream that is remembered bears a message—even the bad ones. Start keeping a pad of paper and a pencil next to your bed. When you awaken from a dream, write something about it—just a word or two will be enough to help you remember. Before going to sleep, ask God to give you the dreams you need, the ones that will strengthen you and make you wiser. Say that you're willing to hear. And then go to sleep and don't worry. God loves you and will give you what you need. Deciding that you are going to start remembering your dreams makes you begin doing so. Figuring out what they may be saying is a rich and important spiritual exercise. Because the part of the mind that dreams is also the part that prays.

Why Geraniums Are the Best-Smelling Flowers on Earth

Why The Geranium Farm, Genevra writes. *They don't smell good.*

What a thing to say about geraniums. Salt of the earth, geraniums: solid citizens of the plant world, faithful friends of humanity. More than a century of service without a murmur in the windows of countless public schools, growing taller and spindlier than most supermodels from straining for the light, neglected over vacations until somebody tosses an offhanded Dixie Cup of water onto their gasping roots. But pinch them down and they set blooms in a day or two, so grateful for the attention that they don't complain about the amputation. Most people should be so stalwart.

They don't smell good. They don't smell good? Geraniums smell *glorious*. They smell of dusty sunlight, of the tangy, spicy energy of life. They eschew the effete sweetness of other flowers, flowers that pander to our indolence. Geraniums smell militantly beautiful, a smell of productivity under extreme circumstances, a smell that says *Don't bother about me, I'll be all right. Take care of the weaker ones.* Geraniums never whine about insects and fungi. They take care of themselves. You don't have to hover over them like an anxious nurse, begging them to grow, feeding them special treats. Not geraniums. *No, no thanks,* they say, *I just ate, really. Couldn't touch another bite.*

Now, there are scented geraniums. Geraniums that claim to smell like lemon, like vanilla, like all manner of lovely things. I'm going to explore them. I found a website about them. There's a price list. But the geraniums here at the Geranium Farm aren't the scented ones, not so far. They are the peppery, solid geraniums of our youth in the public schools, our first jobs in old offices with tall windows where nothing else will grow, of milk cartons filled with potting soil and a little plant to take home on Mother's Day, of cuttings in a glass sending forth white roots in just two days. They are the geraniums of our grandmothers. They, themselves, are grandmothers, some of them: tough and woody of stem, scarred from countless prunings, still sending forth bright blooms, still seeking the light.

I like their smell. I also like the smell of marigolds, another tough one, and of chrysanthemums. These are flowers through whom you can smell the dirt. And all of us come from the dirt. And all of us are heading back there. Thanks be to God, for giving us a season here under the sun. Reach for it while you can.

The Giver and the Gift

I guess we need to find an alarm clock somewhere, Q says. We are visiting his daughter. There is no clock in our room.

Oh, no, I say airily. We can just use mine.

By that I mean my biological clock. I can resolve to wake up at a given hour and do so, within five or ten minutes. All I have to do is look at the time right before I go to sleep, and the inner computer does the rest, I guess. So I never set an alarm. And I never oversleep.

Of course, there's a first time for everything. I believe Q wishes we didn't have to place such utter faith in my inner alarm, that we could accept some help from outside on occasion, such as times when we are in a town in a time zone other than our own, obligated to appear at a certain time to do something for people whom we don't know, early in the morning after a day of airports and disarranged routine.

That is why I went to town this morning to find a travel alarm clock to give him for Father's Day. He shouldn't have to experience any discomfort because I want to show off my inner alarm clock. And, truth, to tell, the old inner alarm isn't what it once was: I find that I awaken hourly for two or three hours before the magic one when I rely on it. That's not exactly restful sleep. I think my innards are telling me not to get too smug about my abilities.

I went to Variety Village, of course. It is the store my kids loved when they were little, and my grandchildren love it, too. What you can buy at Variety Village: hideous flags with tulips or hobgoblins on them to hang on your house. Potting soil. Discontinued brands of nylons. Plastic toys. Artificial flowers. Shampoo. Odd lots of best-selling books from two years ago. Shower curtains. Candles in strange colors. Charcoal lighter. Bleach. Clothespins. Rubber sandals. Baseball cards. Cheap radios. A book entitled *The Many Achievements of the Clinton Administration,* with pictures of Bill and Hillary not looking at each other on the cover. Pencils and erasers and composition books. Thread. Greeting cards. Candy. Dishpans. Curtain rods. Petroleum jelly. Stickers. String. And clocks.

They had a travel alarm, of course. I knew they would. It is small and slim and has its own little case. They got the battery started for me. When I got it home, I met Q bringing in an anonymous box containing the other present I had ordered for him and forgotten about, an ice cream maker. Oops. Well, it will be nice to have. We can make sorbet with it.

He's not the easiest to buy for. He doesn't like things that just take up space. He doesn't like gifts that seem generic, that seem not to be meant for him. Gift-giving opportunities remind him that we live in a country that encourages us to substitute shopping for human interaction, and he doesn't like it.

From a spiritual perspective, gift giving *is* interesting. There are lots of ways to celebrate besides giving presents: dancing, singing, dressing up in fine clothing, eating, setting off fireworks, having a parade. The 18th century didn't know about Christmas presents. In India, you are the one who *gives* gifts on your birthday: you don't get them. The gift-giving holidays are the ones that have come to be about relationships—they weren't always. The gift has come to represent the relationship to us: we think we can measure it just by looking at the price tag.

This impoverishes us. A price tag is external to me. It represents nothing about me at all, only whether I have money or not. For a gift to symbolize our relationship, it should *say* something about you and me. Something might be quite perfect and cost not much at all, if it's about a moment together, a shared idea, a shared love of something. I'm pretty sure about the clock, but I have a mind to go and buy some chocolate truffles, just in case the ice cream maker isn't a direct hit. If ever there was a perfect fit between gift and recipient, it's Q and chocolate.

A Monday Sabbath

I heard on the radio that a company, formerly named in such a way that its connection with Enron was clear, has changed its name—it's now called Monday. Now, you certainly won't make money today calling yourself anything to do with Enron—*Caligula* would probably be better—but Monday?

Most people don't like Mondays. More people have heart attacks on Monday mornings than on any other day of the week—so take it easy on yourself this morning, okay? Don't forget to say your prayers, even a little tiny one, because who knows, you may need one.

The week stretches out before us on Monday. It looks eternal from here, ages and ages until blessed Friday. If work is painful right now—and even jobs we love can be painful indeed—it looks even longer. You can feel more like an insignificant cog in somebody else's wheel on a Monday than on any other day.

I remember Mondays at St. Clement's, though. I often bought a bunch of flowers for the office on Mondays. They were often quieter days than other days. Not quite so many people coming in. A chance to straighten things up after a busy Sunday, a time to reflect upon how the service went, a time to connect with people who seemed to need a call yesterday, even if I didn't know quite why. When the eMos began, a little more than a year ago, the Monday eMo was fun to write—I usually hadn't done one on the weekend, and it pleased me to think of everyone opening it and reading it. It felt like we were all together, all quiet, all thinking our thoughts in quiet community.

The sisters up at the Community of the Holy Spirit on 113th Street have obligations on Sundays that make Sunday not a very quiet day. Instead, they proclaim Monday as their Sabbath. They don't answer the phone, emails, make appointments, cook meals for guests. It's a day to think and pray, to take a walk or a swim, to read or chat, to draw. It's a Sabbath. It doesn't matter when your Sabbath is—Seventh Day Adventists have erected a religion on an absolute conviction that the Sabbath is supposed to be Saturday and that the consequence of having it on another day are terrible, and I say God bless 'em—but any day can be your Sabbath Day.

Sabbath for the sisters is not just a day off. It's a day off in community—everyone is resting and refreshing. That's what's good about Sabbath—we're not just not working, we're resting in community, connecting with God, refreshing ourselves. We're doing these things on a day set apart for them by our community. We're together taking part in God's plan—a day of rest, you'll recall, is in the Employees' Handbook of our faith. Even God took one.

Sundays at St. Clement's were frantic: many services, many requests for time and attention. For me, the Sabbath began with Evening Prayer on Sunday night—a quiet service of song and Scripture, quiet prayer, a simple meal taken together afterward, then a night of well earned sleep. Even when I arrived on Mondays, the Sabbath feel continued. This is a new week. We can begin again. We can begin slowly and quietly. We can make a fresh start.

Open for Business

The "Change Something" office is over—I ditched the blue-check curtains and now have a pair of translucent, pure white panels. So the place looks a lot less frantic, there's air in here now, and I no longer feel like the Swedish lady on the Target billboard.

I can also see the tree outside the window. I can see its trunk, I mean—it's an old evergreen, and its branches have risen high above the house to find some light. Here on the second floor, it's mostly trunk I'm looking at—the branches are high above me. Jenny the Cat used this tree, in her salad days, to climb up to the very roof pole of the house, where she would howl for my husband to come and get her. I always felt she had a rescue fantasy about him.

Now she sleeps at the bottom of her tree—she left this world on Christmas morning, and her tree seemed the right place to put her. I suppose she's off on the next of her nine lives now, and I hope it will be as pleasant as this one was.

We miss Jenny, but it is true that even sad things bring opportunities with them. Jenny was quite a hunter in her day, and now that she's gone, I have become very interested in birds. They come to our feeders in the back. We got them a birdbath the other day—nobody's taken any baths yet, but it's there when they get to feeling scuzzy. We got a very dumb-looking hummingbird feeder, red with big yellow flowers on it, said to be attractive to hummers, which we fill with sugar water every other day. No hummers yet, either, but perhaps if we build it, they will come.

It occurs to me now that I could rig up a feeder on a pulley outside this second floor window. I could throw a line over a branch and haul the feeder up and down to fill it. There's no cat lying in wait for them now. I think I'll do that.

But how will the birds find out about it? They're not used to finding sunflower seeds up here in the sky. How will it ever occur to them to look?

The answer to that is that I don't know how they will do it. I don't even know *if* they will do it. But I do know that, if I do nothing, nothing new will happen. If I do something, it may. Sounds like doing something is a better bet.

So the "Change Something" office is history. It's made way for "Do Something." Sometimes you have to change something in order to do something, I guess. Off to the bird place to find a feeder.

Take Nothing For Granted

Amid all the anguishes in the days after the bombing of the World Trade Center, the possibility of others crept in: who died there that I don't know about yet? I was worried about my late brother's colleagues at the *Journal of Commerce*. I wouldn't have been called—we weren't close friends who saw each other every day—but I didn't relish finding out in five years that one of them had died there and I hadn't known. I called Win Peacock down at John Heuss House, a drop-in center for the mentally ill homeless. Lots of his folks used to drift in and out of the World Trade Center. *No,* he said, *We didn't lose anybody. They're all accounted for.* That's something of a miracle.

People you're not intimate with. People who are just familiar faces, a nod on the street, a brief hello. The same guy every day in the grocery store where you buy the *Times*. The lady at the coffee cart. The mailman. The guy who comes to fix the copy machine. People on the edges of your life. They come to mean more to you than you imagine, and the only way you ever know that is when they are gone.

Remember the guy in a motorized cart, parked every day at the entrance to the Trade Center, corner of Liberty and Church Streets? He had cerebral palsy; I think he had a sign affixed to his chair proclaiming that. He sold pencils. Sometimes he had an able-bodied man with him. He was always there.

Was he there that morning? Where is he now?

Love well that which thou must lose ere long, Shakespeare advises. He's talking about our intimates, of course, the giant figures in our lives, those whose leaving cuts deep wounds in us that take years to heal, and never really do, not completely. But love well those at the edge of your life, too. We live together in the commons of the world, and the loss of even one diminishes us all.

On the way to wherever I'm going, I always choose a stranger or two for whom to pray. I just look at them, study them a bit, glean what I can from what I see—their attire, their facial expressions, their posture. And then I join them in the strong clear river of God's love. It is a mighty river, and we are all in it. I see them in it, and I see myself with them. We are together, carried by its strong, good current. And then the subway door closes, or I leave the little store, and they are gone. We will never meet again on this earth.

But we will meet again in another place. And we will know each other.

All We Can Do Now Is Pray

Sometimes the time zones are not our friends.

Waking up these days can be a painful thing if you follow the news. The day is no longer young in the Holy Land when we awaken in New York—they've had time to kill each other for hours over there. It seems we were just about to announce a peace proposal and put some grit behind it—just going to do it yesterday, apparently—and then the second suicide bombing in as many days put an end to it. Now the horrible cycle begins again: bomber, tanks, bomber, tanks, bomber, more tanks. Pray for the peace of Jerusalem, the psalmist sings. Prayer is all that's left.

Interesting that we say it that way: *All we can do now is pray.* As if it were another way of saying there's no hope. As if prayer weren't much, weren't really doing anything.

And it's true that prayer isn't like shopping. You don't just put in your order and wait for it to arrive. And then—what? Take it back if it doesn't fit?

No, it's not like that. Praying over situations in which you have no more moves is how we allow God to take us into the future. We are like those cheap wind-up toys you can buy: wind them up and set them down, and when they run into a barrier they just keep chugging and pushing in a direction they can't go. We do that. We keep trying to do things that have proven they can't be done in the manner we attempt, and we can't back up. We just keep chugging ineffectually, attempting to go forward and going exactly nowhere.

The toy works again when we pick it up and put it in another place. Then it chugs along on its way. Prayer does that for us. It reorients our striving. It sets us on a path into the future. It helps us stop doing the same useless thing over and over and over again, hoping each time for a different result. You don't get different from same. You get same.

How does prayer do this? It needs, first, to be quiet prayer. Probably wordless prayer. Too many words and, before you know it, you're off and running and telling God how to fix things, when you've just demonstrated that you don't know how. So this prayer in the face of a hopeless cause must be a prayer of listening, a prayer of lifting the sadness of it to God and waiting, a prayer focusing on opening the heart to hear something new, not something old.

History only moves forward. No human situation endures. All of them change. The Middle East will not always be as it is. Something is coming, and we don't know what. But those who revere that Holy Land, who love it and pray for it, must not give up hope. You must not give up hope in any situation that seems hopeless. God is always the one who brings life out of death. That's who God is. *All we can do now is pray.* That may be all we can do. But now we wait and see what God can do.

Active Nouns and Verbs

Q and I went to his fraternity brother's fiftieth wedding anniversary yesterday. What a lovely occasion. I'm looking forward to ours—Q will be 110 years old, and I guess I'll be dead.

"Marry" is an active verb, the bride said. You don't just marry someone one day and then you're married. You marry him or her every day. Every day. It's not a thing you just *are.* It's a thing you do.

Hmmn. Clearly works for them. What about for everyone else? Are other things, things that we think of as walks of life, just ways of identifying ourselves in a passive way, also active? Do we *do* them new every day, rather than *being* them without thinking? Are they continually being renewed rather than happening once and then just becoming a permanent state of affairs?

I think so. Priesthood is active—you really can't just *be* a priest. You have to *exercise* priesthood, choose it every day. Every minute, sometimes, when the going gets rough. Teaching: you can't just *be* a teacher; you *teach.* You teach every day. You teach every student, and every teaching moment is a new one. You can't go onstage and just *be* an actor; you have to go out there and *act.* Every scene is new, even if you've done it a thousand times. When an actor can't keep it new, the show suffers.

I want to be a writer, people sometimes say. Fine. *Write.*

Joe the bartender looks up and sees the same guy coming into the bar for the millionth time. It's the same bar. It's the same guy. Joe's the same guy. But the moment is new. Joe's a bartender. But he can't just *be* one. He has to *tend* the bar. Tend: *to care for, to nourish and improve.* Joe: it's the bartending moment. Enjoy.

Maybe there's nothing we do of any importance at all that we do not actually *tend*. Maybe if we do not *tend,* our walk of life is flat and sad in our experience, instead of rich. Maybe anything can be rich, if we will only *tend* it.

Good morning, Bartender, Churchtender, Childtender, Gardentender, Friendtender. Good morning, Computertender, Sidewalktender, Wordtender. Good morning.

Choosing Life

I was surprised: yesterday, by a vote of 7–2, the Supreme Court set aside more than 150 death sentences. Turned out they were in states where it was possible for a judge alone, rather than the jury, to hand down a death sentence after a conviction. This denies the convicted person his right to trial by jury, they said.

Several states have imposed moratoria on executions—too many mistaken verdicts, sending people to their deaths for crimes they did not commit. Turns out the people executed for crimes of which they were later proven innocent number in the hundreds since the penalty was reinstated. No chance to get it right on a retrial if the defendant's already dead.

Slowly, the tide is turning. It may be that we will one day rejoin the rest of the international company we usually keep. As it is, the group of nations that have and use the death penalty is a motley crew, including Libya, Red China, Saudi Arabia, Syria, Nigeria....and us, of course. This is why other nations scratch their heads when our leaders talk about the importance of human rights.

I know that those who favor the death penalty think that those of us who oppose it don't really understand how terrible some crimes are. That we don't know anything about the longing for revenge. I know *all* about the longing for revenge. I feel it several times a day. When I read of a cruel act and imagine myself meting out justice to the one who committed it—as I usually do—my imagining is graphic and lurid.

I have these feelings of violent longing for revenge and admit to them. I think everyone has them, though not all religious people feel free to say they do—or even to *know* they do! But they are *feelings.* They're not carefully thought-out beliefs. They are primitive parts of me, parts that should be acknowledged, but which should not be allowed to run my life and make my decisions for me.

Human beings are not just one thing. We are not just a bag of feelings. We are also reason, and memory, and will. All of these faculties make us human, and each has its own area of activity. I don't use my emotions to solve a math problem. All the parts of us work together. The same one can't lead all the time.

So, I may have extravagant revenge fantasies about someone who has hurt someone else, but I can't make my moral decisions on the basis of my fantasies. I have to use more of my self. Otherwise, I am like the killer: he doesn't use all of himself, either.

In the end, life is not ours to give or take. It always comes to an end, and measures to prolong it beyond all possibility of its joy do no honor to the sanctity of it, but it is not ours to end before it is over. It is not the murderer's right, and it is not ours.

Who Will Win?

The Yanks lost and the Mets won.

The British lost. Brazil won.

Mexico lost to its enormous next-door neighbor and resented it. The enormous neighbor itself felt like an underdog, something the good old U.S. of A. doesn't know much about being, and it was good for us to be grateful just to be included instead of thinking we run everything.

Nobody knows what's going to happen at Wimbledon.

Most of us think Tiger Woods will win wherever he plays.

Q and I arm-wrestled briefly, yesterday, just to see. I lost.

You win some and you lose some. Recently—I mean recently as in the last twenty years, not the last twenty minutes—we have begun to feel reluctant to focus on winning and losing in what we teach our kids. Games that are not about victory or loss in an adversarial event have appeared, and a skittishness about giving grades has arisen among concerned educators. Why? Because people go crazy if they think there's a competition. They'll drug for that gold medal, foul another player without thinking twice, cheat for that A+, plagiarize for that Pulitzer. Is it a competition? Is there a prize? If so, all's fair.

But people who *don't* want be cutthroat competitors have an uphill battle. It's hard in our culture not to want to win more than you want anything else. The biggest rewards really *do* go to the bloodthirsty competitors. If you elect not to be one, you really *are* saying no to some things it would be nice to have. Is that okay?

It takes spiritual maturity to understand who we are and what that means about what we should do. It requires a modest sacrifice of what everything in the culture encourages us to want: lots of money, an impressive office signifying a high place in the corporate pecking order, a house the size of a small town.

It also takes the cultivated ability to live in the moment. Instead of "What will this get me," it requires me to ask myself "Where am I right now, and how do I like it?" Somewhere along the line, we must stop conquering and live. Somewhere along the line, we must begin to ask ourselves this question: If my life were to be over tomorrow, would I have lived enough to leave this world without resentment?

We can't control how long our lives will be. But we're the only ones who decide how full they will be.

Still No Hummers

Every two days, without fail, I boil two cups of water with half a cup of sugar and let it cool. While it's cooling, I go outside and get the dumb-looking hummingbird feeder we bought a couple of weeks ago and clean it with fresh water. You have to supply a clean batch of nectar—that's what the sugar water is, *nectar*—and clean the container, so the hummingbirds won't get a germ.

What hummingbirds?

As faithful as I have been, as garish a red as the feeder is, as dumb-looking as the yellow flowers on it are—not a hummer has visited our feeder. It swings enticingly in the breeze, and other birds have taken to using it for a perch. But no hummers have come.

I remember church being like that sometimes. We would knock ourselves out over some project, and it would be really wonderful. Really worthwhile. And we would hope for a gratifying response. And we would get something else. It was hard to keep on keeping on sometimes.

But you have to keep on. You can't give up trying, although you may need to change your strategy. You may need to stop insisting that it be done a certain way, and try a new way. But you have to keep trying for the good you seek. One of the hardest things about doing something new is finding the way in which to do it best, the way that fits you. Your way will be a little different from someone else's way. No two places and no two people are just the same.

Talking with a friend the other day, I mentioned the birds. He has hummers, he says, four or five of 'em sometimes. They'll come, he says. You just have to be patient.

I am being patient. More patient than I have ever been. I know the hummingbirds will come. I'll keep cleaning their feeder and making new, sweet nectar. Maybe I'll get a couple of other feeders and put them in other places around the yard, so that the hummers will think it's a convention. However it happens, one day I'll look out and there one will be, her wings beating so fast they are nothing but a silvery blur, her body an amazing iridescent green. I know she will come. Living in expectation of her appearance is already a happy thing.

Therefore With Angels

Let's go to the Cornerstone for dinner, I said to Q, *and hear some music.*

The food at the Cornerstone is nothing special, although my pasta was decent. Q's veal Marsala has been on the menu there for twenty years, at least, and is more innocent of sherry than a dish going by that name ordinarily is. I reminded him about the French dressing on his salad: I knew he assumed it would be an interesting, herby vinaigrette, and explained that, instead, it would arrive fresh from the bottle, a sweet bright orange cream of a sort never consumed in France.

Checking the chalkboard to see who was playing, I was surprised to see that Thursdays were blank. Thursday used to be a big night. *No music tonight?* I asked the waitress. *Well, on Thursdays we have Frank on the piano now and, uh, it's open-mike,* she said, smiling indulgently and gesturing toward several tables full of older people. *I don't want to scare you.*

We weren't scared. I had entertained hopes for some good jazz—most people don't know about jazz in Metuchen, but we do have some. No matter. It was raining outside, and our salads had already arrived. And soon Frank sat down at the piano and began to play "It Might As Well Be Spring." And then he called John up, telling us that John was a WWII veteran who had been in a POW camp, and that John would sing "God Bless America," and everybody clapped. And John did, and so did everybody else. John is eighty-three. He doesn't sound bad.

Then George was up, with two more standards, and then a cheerful woman in a pretty blue dress. And another guy, and another. A young woman sang a torch song for which she was not suited and then two show tunes that showed where her heart and her talent really was. The waiters brought out a cake for Anna Maria's birthday and everybody sang "Happy Birthday," and then a friend of hers sang the traditional Polish birthday song, which has a completely different tune. People came and went, and Frank gave us a number or two on the piano in between.

"I wonder if these people were friends before they started coming here or became friends here," I said to Q.

"Could have been either way, I guess," he said. We were finishing the meal with coffee. A large man was recovering his tenor range on "The Tennessee Waltz." Singers who had had their moment tablehopped, congratulating each other on their performances.

A sweet evening, innocently sweet: people singing for one another, singing together. Remembering a time when they were young and bringing it back. Using voices that have changed over the years, discovering what they can and can't do now, tolerating their own limitations and those of others. Singing songs everybody knows.

It has been assumed from the earliest days that people sing in heaven. We allude to it in the Eucharist: *therefore we praise you, joining our voices with angels and archangels, who forever sing this hymn to proclaim your holy Name*. They sing all the time. Even here on earth, it's pretty hard to remain sad when you sing, and there is a music for every emotion of which human beings are capable.

Not everybody last night sang well, although some of them sang very well indeed. But the important thing about singing isn't always that you sing well. Sometimes it's that you sing at all.

It Is Never Too Late To Begin

Actually, today the eMo is not from the Geranium Farm at all. Nor is it from the St. Clement's-in-the-'Hood. I am in Kentucky, here to officiate in the baptism of Brayden Romeo Roberge, who became a Christian yesterday at St. Francis in the Fields near Louisville. One of the great pleasures of ordained ministry is that you get to baptize the children of people you marry.

Actually, you get to be a part of every turning point in life. Sadder, but still satisfying, is the privilege of attending the illness of someone with whom and through whom you have served Christ—and, eventually, attending that person's death, being one of the people who stands at the foot of the cross upon which we will all, one day, be lifted high.

Of course, what an ordained minister does is really not different from what everyone is called to do. I know many lay people who know the rich, draining mix of joy and sorrow that ministry to the sick carries with it. Many of us, lay and ordained, have been privileged to be the one through whose dependable presence someone was able to leave this world in peace and not alone. It is not the mystery of ordination that confers ministry on a person—it is the mystery of baptism itself. Or, to be perfectly honest, it is probably really only the mystery of being born a human being that calls us to serve.

Brayden was his customary serene self during his baptism. He wondered only a bit at the threefold splash of water on his head—I don't think anyone heard him asking about it but me. People who loved him—his parents, his uncle, his grown-up cousin—promised to help him become the man God created him to be. He has made a good start—Buddha-like in his good humor and peacefulness, full of quiet delight when his dad makes faces at him, eager to stand and walk, even though he is not yet old enough to begin doing so.

They promised, on his behalf, that he would, when he fell into sin, repent and return to the Lord. We all promised that, together. We were the ones who really needed the reminder, not Brayden: he hasn't had a chance to sin yet. The rest of us, though, know a lot about what it is to fall down, to be ashamed of our conduct, to wish we had done something differently, to regret. We saw him washed of sins he has not committed and remembered that we, too, can begin again on the ones we *have*.

They said on the radio that the biggest wildfire in Arizona history was set by a firefighter—he needed the work. How strange—the terrible one in Colorado seems to have been a firefighter's arson, too. Two people whose job it is to save and preserve, causing death and destruction. Two ashamed people, who knew better and did it anyhow. The young man said he was sorry—the judge quickly hushed him up. Saying you're sorry is not a good thing to do when you're a defendant. But it's a very good thing to do for a human being. It's the only way to begin the road back.

I believe him when he says he's sorry. Believe him, and treasure the beginning he has made of repentance. He'll still have to face the consequences of his action—our actions have consequences, and they belong to us alone. But his repentance brings him back into our midst when his action had taken him out of it, and in the name of God we welcome him, and anyone who repents, back into the family. That welcome is what being a Christian means. It is never too late to begin.

You Have Today

Now, listen up, people: we're supposed to be vigilant, but *relaxed.*

We are of two minds about whether we want to be warned about what the FBI learns, since it is never anything definite. Something may happen. *What? Where? When?* Nobody knows.

We react to this uncertainty with the usual response: outrage. *Whaddya mean, nobody knows?!?* We experience the lack of specificity as a personal annoyance, like when the cable guy doesn't come. We want to know which bridge is threatened, and exactly when the attack is scheduled, so we can plan the weekend.

It appeared, at first, that we would understand ourselves to be part of the world now, that we would finally *get* the fact that life is terribly uncertain and always has been. Our privileged position was over. We would understand what many people in many countries have understood for a long time: there really is such a thing as the wrong place and the wrong time, and there is a limit to the amount of engineering one can do to counter that fact.

But we are Americans: even now, after all that has happened, it is hard for us to believe that we may not triumph with ease every time. We have forgotten the terrible tedium of war. Some of us have never known it. We have learned to expect our technological skill to provide us with a speedy resolution to everything. The confidence that makes us productive also has a shadow side: it weakens us, impairs our endurance. We do ourselves no favor when we expect ease.

Immediately after the bombing, a nation turned to God. Being us, of course, we did it noisily: plastic flags, horrid "Dead or Alive" posters, way too much Irving Berlin. God being God, though, our crassness was not the only word spoken: people who had never known the joy of service discovered it. People who had forgotten their faith got it down from the shelf and dusted it off, and found that it still fit. The continuing toll of the dead and the continuing recovery of their remains bore eloquent testimony to what treasures life and love are. Our adolescent attention span and pettishness when we are denied does not drown out these things, not completely.

Human life is uncertain and always has been. An exception has not been made in our case. Human life is hard—harder than many of us may have thought, harder than we may know yet. Life may be hard, but God is good.

What will happen? We don't know. Will we have tomorrow? There is no guarantee. But we have today, right now, a gift that is ours to open and use. It is the only today we will ever have. Endure, survive and become stronger from what is hurtful in it. Savor and delight in what is good.

Machines in Hell

It is amusing, in a quiet way, that I publish an electronic serialized book—that's what the eMos are, by the way: they'll be coming out in a *book*, the kind with pages you can turn, at the end of the year. *It's not amusing, it's a miracle,* Bobby Hecht would say. Bobby used to sit with me in the office at St. Clement's and patiently walk me through sending email that never went anywhere. He used to walk over to the desk where I sat and swore, unable either to make the thing work or to turn it off, and he would peer at the frozen screen. Then he would take a ballpoint pen or a paper clip and stab it into an unlabeled screw on the front of the console—and it would obediently shut off so we could try again.

"What the hell did you do?"

"It's like *control-alt-delete*," he would say, returning to his chair. "It's an old trick. A lot of people don't know about it."

Sometimes computers can't take it any more. They just stop—screen immobile, mouse nowhere to be found, keyboard firmly unrelated to anything happening in the box, unable even to connect long enough to turn the thing off. A sterile motor hum, but no interesting rustle of hardware—it's not doing anything.

Now, we all know that feeling. There are times when we come to the end of the day somewhat in advance of its being over, when we simply shut down and can't—won't—move. *Bartleby the Scrivener*, Herman Melville's odd story of work and homelessness on Wall Street in the 1840s, has an office worker like that: his boss asks him to copy this or that, to do this or that, and he has but one reply:

"I would prefer not to."

Oh, yeah. I know those moments. You do too. Sometimes the spine of duty wilts right out of us, and we say the hell with it. For a little while.

And computers do too, I guess. Within them, as I understand it, are multiple options to accomplish any one action. They scan over the available paths until they find one that's free and clear, start down it and you see what you're expecting on your screen. But sometimes they look and look, and all the paths are blocked—by what, I wonder—and they get bored with the search. I know just how they feel.

Long ago, I was part of their search. I was a keypunch girl. Many people don't remember keypunch girls—we seemed to be *only* girls, and newspapers advertised for us that way—but you may. We sat at large machines—about the width of a piano keyboard—and loaded rectangular cards into one end of them. Then we typed a meaningless jumble of letters, numbers and symbols that we got from a long roll of computer paper that hung on a rack to our left, and the machine would punch holes in the cards according to the characters we typed. Each card was a step in the flow of actions that comprised the computer program. It would tell the machine which path to take, but we knew none of this: we just typed the jumble of letters and numbers, over and over. At the end of our task, we would hand a three-or-four-inch stack of punctured cards to the boss. Nothing would work if even one card were out of order. Your PC does all this itself now, so you don't have to. Think about that next time it wants to take a little nap, and try to be understanding.

Keypunch technology is now obsolete. Thank God. Look in the Help Wanted—no keypunch girls needed. All of us are now doctors and lawyers and biochemists and stand-up comediennes. One of us is a priest. I've always wondered where all those enormous and very heavy machines went. What did they do with them? And where are all the cards? Laid end to end, they would reach to the moon and back many, many times.

I think I know where they went.

They're in hell. Keypunch is a significant demographic in the world of work there, thousands, perhaps millions of keypunch girls—and boys, now—sitting at the scorching machines and typing @<<*dkv^jnw(ro)pijh* >>. The cards burst into flames as soon as each program is completed, and a devil comes by and pokes you with his fork: you have to start the whole program again. One program lasts you the whole of eternity, and you can't even change with the person next to you.

You do *not* want to go there. For your own good, behave yourselves.

God Set Them in a Garden

I was in Charlotte, North Carolina, preaching at Connie Connelly's ordination to the priesthood. She was one of our seminarians at St. Clement's. It was an honor to be a part of her great day—she glowed with happiness when the red chasuble was settled over her shoulders, like a Roman bride—they wore red, not white, you know. I had dreamed half the sermon. In the dream, I was somehow responsible for capturing numerous birds of different varieties, and enclosing them in a hinged box. It was hard, catching the birds, and every time I lifted the hinged lid to put one in, another one got out. I was struggling and losing the battle—one fragile white bird got caught on the edge of the lid, and hurt herself there: she fluttered weakly to a branch out of my reach and hung dangerously from it by one broken wing. Oh, no—*I had hurt her.* Another bird—a hummingbird, no less—got away and was stranded way up on the very top of our roof. Now what? Everything was going wrong.

My husband appeared. He went up on the roof and got the hummingbird. And a gardener appeared—*I didn't know we had a gardener.* The gardener went to the branch and carefully lifted the wounded bird away from it, gave me a reassuring nod and walked away with it. Somehow, I knew the bird would now be healed.

Then one of those authoritative that's-the-way-it-is voices that sometimes come in dreams said to me, "This is a dream about the priesthood."

It is? I said. I didn't see it. But I always listen to what I am told in dreams.

In real life, we arrived in North Carolina the day before the ordination. "Are you going with us?" Connie asked in the morning. Going where? To Wing Haven, she said, a garden with birds here in Charlotte.

To a garden.

Oh. Yeah, I guess I'm going. This is probably where I'll find out about the dream. In time to preach the sermon.

Wing Haven began in 1926, the dream of a couple married in that year. They began to dig in barren red clay the day after they married. They never had children: for birthdays and Christmases, they gave each other birdbaths, plants, bricks. The garden grew. As they found money, they bought adjoining lots and enlarged their garden. Brick paths wandered through it, banks of lavender, stands of lilies, beds of herbs. You behold a fountain in the distance and pass great beauty as you walk toward it, and then you look in another direction and see another one.

At first, nearer the house, the garden is planned and somewhat formal. As it progresses, though, and you walk further and further away from the house into it, it becomes wilder. The brick walks are gone; the paths are made of wood chips instead. The cultivated beds of flowers are gone; instead, it is like a wood, a place where animals can feel and be their wild selves. You can tell that the people who loved the garden changed over the years, came to see themselves more and more as ones who supported the lives of the animals, rather than as ones who subdued the plants of the earth. Became less designers, more friends.

Oh. *Oh.*

You don't have to put birds in a box to keep them safe. Birds can fly. They're okay where they are. Plants already know how to grow. Animals already know what to do. And so do the people of God—they don't need someone to protect them from life, to manage and design their lives for them. That's not what a priest does. They just need someone to support and encourage them to live a whole and holy life themselves, in the way they know how. Make sure the things they need are there—plants, seeds, water, trees, a little underbrush—and animals can take it from there. They will come because they can find what they need.

And we are the same. Healthy community is intrinsically attractive. People naturally want to be there and naturally want to help it grow and flourish. It is love in community for which we were created—by a God who, at the beginning of things, we say, set us in a garden and gave us what we needed.

Strong and Healthy

Back at the gym.

Hey! Long time no see! I say to the trainer, whom I remember from before I let my membership lapse.

Well, I've *been here,* she says. Uh, yeah. I knew one of us was missing.

Back to the circuit of machines. I used to just about live here. Came here every day, at 5:30 in the morning sometimes. Nine p.m. other times. Loved it. Loved competing with myself, lifting more and more weight. Loved how it made me feel: strong and healthy. Both *strong* and *healthy* have been scarce for the last couple of years. I should have realized I was headed for trouble when I let my gym membership lapse. *No time for it,* I told myself. I should have seen statements like that as the dangerous signals they were, along with having trouble with stairs and feeling weak and sad all the time. I would return home at night too exhausted to consider going to the gym, although I knew that getting the right amount of exercise would have given me more, not less energy. I filled every day with obligations that insured I would have no time for the gym or anything else that I needed. And I suffered the consequences one would expect.

Yesterday I started out with the weights where I had left off with a couple of years ago. Big mistake: I'm not the person I was a couple of years ago. Today I walk even funnier than usual. I'll let it heal up until tomorrow and try again, this time at a more old-lady level, in keeping with my approaching cronedom.

Maybe this time I'll do things a little differently. I loved piling on the weights, lifting more and more. I always wanted to increase my load. I think I was showing off to myself. But now I begin to question that as a philosophy of life: maybe sometimes we're supposed to *decrease* our load. If you lift a lot of weight, you need fewer repetitions of each exercise. If you don't lift quite so much, you can do more reps. Maybe that's what I'll do this time. Maybe I won't be in such a hurry. I loved it before. Maybe I'll love it even more, because now I know how hard it is to be weak and ill, and how good it is to feel better. Maybe the relationship between my own behavior and my own happiness will feel more like they have something to do with each other. Maybe my health will come to feel less like an accident and more like a practice.

That would be good.

Lunch With John Adams

I'll walk over to the West Side, I said to myself, and have lunch somewhere with John Adams. I am currently immersed in the five-pound, forty-dollar biography of our second president. I would find a French restaurant; I was just then reading about his first visit to France: a perilous crossing of the Atlantic, a diplomatic visit conducted by a non-French speaker on behalf of a nation which barely existed, his little boy along with him on the dangerous, exciting trip.

I set off from Gramercy Park, where I had just finished the mass at Calvary Church. All the French places were busy—Bastille Day. I ended up at Chelsea Commons on Tenth Avenue, an old haunt of mine from seminary days. It had not so much as a *croque monsieur* on the menu. But it was quiet and cool, and I could read undisturbed.

The French Revolution was still a decade away when Adams arrived in Paris. He was there to enlist French alliance in the war for independence, just beginning—and not going very well—back home across the sea. Eighteenth-century communication being what it was, he alighted in France to find that the alliance had already been secured; the work he had come to do was basically done. Still, there were friendships to be formed and an amazing society to be understood. The first person Adams called on was his own countryman: old Benjamin Franklin, his famous colleague in the Continental Congress, who had been the darling of French society for ages.

The French were fascinated with the Americans. Franklin, especially, they loved: his simple clothes, his plain hair contrasted exotically with their satins and laces, their wigs and jewels. His aristocratic admirers would not have been so enthusiastic about their foreign visitors had they appeared a dozen years later: our revolution offered encouragement to theirs, and theirs made ours look like a Sunday school picnic. The French Revolution was a cataclysmic reordering of society, unleashing centuries of hidden fury and revising a whole society in a matter of months. The storming of the Bastille symbolized the end of the brutal power of the king. But the revolution it inaugurated was followed by something whose name says quite enough: The Reign of Terror.

Human events don't always turn out as they are imagined beforehand. Large events and small ones, nations and individuals: you start something and it ends up in a place where you would never in a million years have wanted to go, and you have to back out, painfully, embarrassingly, and try as best you can to clean up the mess you made. The unintended consequences of our actions, if laid end to end, would be even more of a pain in the neck than they already are.

Those were tumultuous days. Revolution, terror, sudden wrenching change, terrible anger, the collision of cultures. Not unlike today. Not unlike all human days. Life here is exhausting. It is often dispiriting.

But it is life. Very early this morning, before the birds were up, the phone rang. It was Greg. When I heard his voice, I knew what had happened. His dad has lingered in the twilight between this world and the next for several weeks now, and he had just crossed over. At the hospital, we saw an old man whose battle was over. He looked so peaceful. No more tubes, no ventilator, no beeping monitors any more. All that is over now.

Life. Good intentions that work out well and good intentions that go awry. Plans that come to pass and plans that must be changed. Hope fulfilled and hope denied.

People who live to a generous old age and people who die much too soon. People at their very worst and people who rise to occasions they never would have thought supportable. Ideas whose time has come. Ideas that cling futilely to the past. Remembering. Forgetting.

In the hospital, the ancient words of the Church's farewell: *Depart, O Christian soul, out of this world, in the Name of God the Father who created you, God the Son who redeemed you, God the Holy Spirit who gave you life....* Before the beginning of this life, before the beginning of this world, before the beginning of all worlds. And after the end of this life, and the world, and all the worlds. From there we came, and to there we return.

How To Iron

My first paying job was ironing. This happened under my grandmother's auspices; she lived with us and managed the house when I was a child. I got a nickel for a shirt and a dime for a sheet. Handkerchiefs I threw in for nothing.

It is in summer that I remember ironing the most—probably things were too busy during the academic year, and I didn't do it. But in summer, the heat outside mingling with the fragrant steam rising from the shirts—a multiplication of heat that I don't remember as oppressive, although it must surely have been considerable—I remember it as a satisfying thing indeed. Laundry is *very* satisfying: a wad of wrinkled, soiled clothing gets another chance, becomes clean and good smelling. Ironing is even better: that which was wrinkled and misshapen becomes smooth and perfect again. This only works with laundry. It shows forth an ideal that, in our bodies, we will never achieve. *Our* wrinkles are here to stay.

There is a way to iron a shirt. It is instructive for straightening out a life, too, and for maintaining one. Here it is:

1. Start with the parts of the shirt that will wrinkle least during the ironing process and get them out of the way. These are the collars, which you do first, then the back yoke if there is one, then the cuffs and then the rest of the sleeve. These parts of the shirt will maintain themselves better while you concentrate on the areas people see most, which are also the parts of the shirt most likely to re-wrinkle. *Let the shape of the task help you decide how to do it.*

2. Do the back of the body next. Then the front pieces. Make sure the area under the buttons is lying flat, or the shirtfront will look lumpy and the buttons may strain. *Understand where stress is coming from and factor it in.*

3. Use steam or sprinkle with water. Sprinkling with water is best. Those dumb-looking soda bottle cork tops with holes in them are making a comeback, or you can use a spray bottle. But you need some water with the heat of the iron to train the fibers to lie in the same direction, fibers which were just trained in the heat and wet of the wash to go every which way. *The elements of disorder are the same as the elements of order. You can choose how they will apply.*

4. Whether you sprinkle or spray, make sure you then iron the area completely dry. Otherwise it will wrinkle up again. Same with spray starch, if you use that. *Finish what you start.*

5. There are new irons out now in transparent gumdrop colors. They are very lightweight, and this is a selling point about them. Wrong. You don't want a light iron. If your iron is light, you have to press harder. Let the iron be heavy, and your arm is saved. So use your mom's old clunker and leave the gumdrop colors where God intended them: on computers. *Youth and beauty are no match for experience and strength.*

Or—you can take all the shirts out to the laundry down the street and let them do it. *There are many worthy tasks in this world. You won't be doing all of them.*

Great Green Goodness

Things got a little out of hand yesterday.

We can stop at the nursery afterward, I said to Q on our way to what I knew would be the first of several futile visits to the Department of Motor Vehicles (never let your driver's license expire). By the time we left the DMV, my seratonin level was dangerously low. I felt like an Enron perp or the Lindbergh kidnapper. I needed to stop at the nursery for a restorative of goodness.

Sure enough: a sale on *cannas,* the impressive tall southern lily with wonderful dark red-veined leaves, large and stiff as billowing sails, with intensely colored yellow or red blooms. In this climate you have to take it in for the winter, but it's well worth it. We got two yellow and a red. And a new plant, new to me, with stems of multiple red trumpet-shaped blooms. Trumpet-shaped: I am always hoping hummingbirds will visit our garden. With our Volkswagen filled with four-foot plants—*Why is there dirt on your ceiling, Mamo?* Madeline would ask later that afternoon—we set out for home, my mood completely restored.

Just past the Superfund site lot I want to buy to make a community garden that will be a wonder of New Jersey, we pass our hardware store. In the summer, the wrenches and paint and plumbing supplies are joined by a profusion of plants for sale in the parking lot. ALL PLANTS HALF PRICE, the sign said. *Hmmmn.* We brought the cannas and their multi-bloomed red friend home. Q started in on some garden work. I sneaked back to the hardware store. It wouldn't hurt to look.

In half an hour, richer by two cutleaf bleeding hearts, an astilbe, three dark-leaved hostas, two four-foot butterfly plants, two blue asters, four blue-and-white delphinia, two variegated balloon flowers, a red day lily and a yellow one, and poorer by $50, I was back, just in time for Frances' lunchtime visit. She pulled in just behind me, took one look at the jungle in the back seat and began to unload plants. *There was a sale,* I said sheepishly. Frances smiled. *If you need some help getting these in the ground,* let me know. This is a good thing. Frances has been a gardener for years, and now lives in an apartment where she gardens on a much smaller scale, in containers. Seeing the jungle of plants made her itch for dirt under her nails, I could tell. I *think* I could tell. If she was just being nice, she was being *awfully* nice. She reached in her car and brought out a lovely pot of purple coleus. That makes twenty-two plants. Then Q heard about the sale and went back for a rose. Twenty-three.

The rose is in, in the big wooden wine barrel—it haughtily displaced two geraniums, who got out of the way and into temporary plastic tubs without a murmur, three leggy pansies, affable but past their prime, and two intrepid portulaca, one of whom was invited back into the wine barrel after the rose was enthroned and the other of whom volunteered for window box duty.

Frances says coming all the way down here at dawn to dig and haul and water and handle worm turds would be a pleasure. I believe her. The next day I'm in New York. I walk west on 113th Street and see a square of weeds at the base of a tree. Impatiens plants peek through here and there, desperate for space. I bend over and weed for a minute or so, place the weeds carefully on the stoop of the apartment building to which the tree belongs—a Columbia faculty house, they really could do better. I wait for a traffic light on the street corner and deadhead a pot of petunias languishing on the corner. I wait for a train and discreetly weed a window box at the station.

One of the signs of Q's mother's early stage Alzheimer's was, in the family lore, that she was apprehended out in front of her Park

Avenue apartment house on her hands and knees in the median strip, dividing plants and weeding as the cars whizzed by. Q tells this story and people shake their heads and smile.

She did have Alzheimer's, and she had it for years. It was awful. There were many sad examples of her terrible impairment. But I have come to believe that gardening in the median on Park Avenue wasn't one of them. It seems perfectly normal to me.

Be Careful What You Think God May Be Saying

A new shrine: the window in my office, through which, in the morning, a cool breeze usually enters. The tree our old black cat Jenny climbed until well into her 17th year is directly outside the window, and a new bird feeder hangs from a branch. It has attracted many new friends: downy woodpeckers, who creep down the trunk upside down, gather courage for a leap to the feeder and then fly off to eat their seed in peace. House wrens of different colors, including one redheaded beauty. Titmice. Warblers. Birds I can't name yet. How lovely.

This is where I read Morning Prayer now. The cool air, the tiny, interesting animals going about their business, singing and scolding. The passing cars, as commuters begin to make their way to the city. And ancient words of prayer, song and story. Right now, in the readings that accompany Morning Prayer, the church is making its way through the slow and painful entry of the children of Israel into the Promised Land. Moses is dead, and Joshua is learning to lead. He's doing pretty well. There's lots of fighting and trickery, lots of suspicion of people outside the community and competitive carrying on within it.

The Israelites triumph over kingdom after kingdom. This has remained with us in these ancient texts, texts to which we are bound by tradition. Texts we say are inspired by God. I read of these ancient battles and turn on the radio: two—almost simultaneous—suicide bombings. I wonder as I listen, as I wonder every day: When will it end?

I'm not sure the best thing that ever happened to the Jewish people was the continuation of the idea that their residence in that place is the irrevocable will of God. That they *own* it, in a way divinely ordained and different from the tenure of other people in other countries. Their sense of being chosen helped them sustain themselves in those early days. The idea of God's choosing encourages the oppressed and helps them survive terrible things. It does something else, though, to those who are in charge. It facilitates an erroneous self-understanding: God chose us, so anything we want to do must be God's will because it's us doing it. The Israelis, of course, are not the only people who have gotten into moral trouble because they think they own the land and nobody else can be there. We almost exterminated our own indigenous people because it seemed so clear to us that God wanted us to have the land instead of them

God probably doesn't "give" people land. We aren't the owners of land. We live on it and it nourishes us, but it is not ours. We want to live on it. But we don't own it. And we needn't go very far along the path of thinking we own it before we find ourselves becoming as territorial as animals in the wild.

The song of the birds begins at about 5 a.m. these days. One starts, and then they all pile in. In most species, only the males sing. They sing for only two reasons: to attract a mate and to warn others off their turf. "This is my yard," they sing, "and if you're a male of my species you'd better beat it right now." Even the birds have turf.

I love their song. But I do not forget that it is partially rooted in violence. I love the Scriptures, too, those old, old stories of human frailty and divine grace. But I do not forget that they, too, sometimes enshrine violence. That the world has changed greatly since their composition. That means we must read them very, very carefully, so that we can discern God's voice within them. God will not speak to us in just the same manner in which he spoke to the writer of the Book of Joshua. God will speak to us about our world, in our own language, with the kinds of thoughts we have in our own era. So be careful, when you think you know exactly, right off the bat, what God is saying to you. It may not be so. God is pretty complicated.

A Natural

I just returned from Florida. Not everyone in New York wants to visit Florida in July, but most of my trips to that state have been in the summer. A dozen years ago, I was going down there all the time, to help found the Seamen's Church Institute of Florida, the first of several offshoots of SCI/New York & New Jersey. Now, SCI of Florida sees more seafarers in a year than any other seafaring ministry in the world.

"I've still got the cigar box that Maria used as a cash register when she first opened up." David said as we drove from the airport. He's the Director of SCI/Fla, and he's also Maria's husband. But he wasn't back then: she was young, single, serious and quietly beautiful. She was a student intern from Madrid, one of many international students I had in those days, and it was immediately clear that she had a chaplain's heart, and that there was nobody else better suited to begin a ministry from scratch in an area where Spanish-speaking seafarers and Spanish-speaking volunteers abounded.

I remember that cigar box. Maria used it to make change for phone calls, the main thing seafarers needed from us. They needed to call home, and there were no cell phones then. In those early days we drove around Miami and Port Everglades, meeting church leaders and maritime officials, people with money and people with enthusiasm and some people with both, trying to interest the locals in the work of caring for a group of people nobody cares much about. Trying to get money. Trying to get a building. My maritime ministry colleague Paul Chapman used to come, too, to twist the arm of his friend Allan Milledge, a Miami lawyer whose iconoclasm seemed not to have interfered with his prosperity, to put us in touch with the people we needed to meet. Paul, handy with tools, built a row of phone booths. Maria and I bought $1,000 worth of furniture from the Door Store. Allan became the chairman of the board. The people he sent to us in Southeast Florida had the same experience of our visits that he did: once they met Maria, they were sold. The Bishop of Southeast Florida opened his heart to us, and that diocese continues to welcome these visitors from all over the world to its shores.

Now SCI/Fla has no cigar-box cash boxes, but it does have many computers, two vans, twenty or more employees, a completely ecumenical ministry, and an appreciative board. When Maria got married, she brought SCI with her as a kind of dowry, and David is the ministry's energetic executive director now. They have a cheerful seafarers' club, with telephones everywhere you look, computers the seafarers can use for free, and a little store, where a seafarer can buy what he needs: razor blades, toothpaste, chewing gum. He can send money home, or play the piano, or have a prayer meeting, or a talk with Maria, or just relax and watch TV away from the ship, his 24-hour-a-day combined home and workplace.

I am so proud of them.

"Do you ever think of leaving the maritime ministry?" I asked Maria as we sat and chatted. Their two children were newly in bed, and quiet. We had not had too much time to talk, just the grownups by ourselves. I am no longer in seafarers' ministry. Paul has retired from it. But Maria remains.

She thought a moment, then smiles and shakes her head. "I've been doing it so long," she said, "It's just my nature now."

I nodded. But it was her nature *then*, too. I think it has always been. Far from home herself, she knew what it was to be alone in a strange country. I remember driving along the waterfront with her once and spotting a ship with a Spanish flag—we didn't get too many Spanish ships. I remember how excited she was to see it, how she turned to me and asked if we couldn't go on board. Of course we could. And she talked animatedly with her countrymen, gesturing gracefully with her hands as they stood around her and heard her welcome, her inquiries about their homeland, where she was from, telling her where they were from. She was a natural.

Who she *is* has informed what she *does*. She is a luminous presence on the waterfront—a place that can sometimes be a little short on luminosity—because she is most herself there. When you can spend most of your time doing that thing which is most you, you are luminous. There is a rightness about going to work. You know you are where you were made to be.

Houseguests

It was time for me to go to the airport. The children of the house skipped outside to say good-bye as I got into the car.

"Don't forget about the pies," Hugo said. We had agreed that we would make two pies on my next visit: strawberry for Anna and chocolate chip for Hugo. My next visit is scheduled for sometime in the spring; this will give me time to invent a chocolate chip pie.

"Take care of your cat," I said to the children. They smiled, and both immediately grabbed hold of the startled cat's tail: we had told a story the night before in which Anna and Hugo could fly by holding onto the tail of their magic cat. It was a great story: they met a sloth, who came to live in their yard, and they procured dinosaurs to ride all the way up the Eastern Seaboard to New York, passing through Washington, where the president came out on the porch of the White House to wave at them, past our house in New Jersey, where Q and I came out on our porch to wave, and into New York, where they crossed Central Park and ended up at FAO Schwartz, in which sacred shrine their magic cat granted them the wish of one toy apiece, anything they wanted.

I remember houseguests when I was little. Sometimes my aunt and uncle came to visit; I was in love with him when I was four—he was a paratrooper in the war, and had lovely black hair in a wave on his forehead. My aunt seemed not to mind my infatuation with her husband; she was glamorous, it seemed to me, more glamorous than my mother, and she smoked pastel-colored cigarettes sometimes.

One summer Mr. Bradbury came to stay: he was a seminary student helping out at our little church, and he had a model of a dinosaur skeleton we loved to look at. Cousin Ruth came several times; she was a nurse, and came and stayed when my grandmother was dying to help my mother care for her.

It was exciting to have strangers in our house. People at the breakfast table who didn't ordinarily eat there, people in their pajamas, people to whom I could show treasures and special places in our house. Anna and Hugo felt that excitement, too. It transforms your house to have someone else sharing it for a day or two.

There's nothing like having a stranger around to make your own place look exciting again. We put out the best for our guests, whatever the best is. In most very poor countries, there is a paradoxically high value put on hospitality—one would think their poverty would make them less willing to welcome the stranger and share, but in fact they are more so, much more hospitable than we ordinarily are here. You see this in the Bible all the time: Abraham and Sarah scrounging the last pita to give to three angels who arrive unannounced, the widow giving Elijah the last of her flour and oil in a special cake—poor, poor people holding nothing back from complete strangers.

It is not only more blessed to give than to receive, it is actually more fun.

Sloths

Some sloths have two toes and some have three. They live in Central America, primarily. They spend almost all their time in the branches of tall trees—they even give birth up there. They only come down once a week, to pee. Believe me, if I had to choose between urinating fifty feet above the ground and giving birth there, I'd be making a different decision than the sloths. But it's their life.

They're so slow, it takes them forty-five minutes to climb back up after their bathroom break—they're most vulnerable to predators at this time, as they can be seen more clearly, and they certainly can't run away from anybody. They move so seldom that a greenish-gray algae grows on their fur. This they eat, thereby saving the energy reaching out for a leaf would require. I respect that.

The way the fur grows on their faces makes them look like they are smiling. For this reason, they are beloved of children all over the world. I know this because I log onto the Sloth Web Site sometimes, and read letters the children have written in about how much they love sloths. Once in a while, I write in to the site myself, in the persona of a sloth. I answer questions about my quiet lifestyle. They tell me they want me for a pet.

I was busy in my last parish—St. Clement's was a busy place. The work never ended, and there was a lot of it. It was all work that needed to be done, and much of it was a pleasure, but it wore me out. I found peculiar solace in the sloths—in thinking about them, looking at pictures of them, reading about them. Their slowness. The narrow limitations of their lives, lives so utterly unlike my own. I had a framed picture of a sloth mother and baby, displayed alongside the framed pictures of my family. I had a small stuffed sloth on my desk. At my last Epiphany pageant at

St. Clement's, I played a sloth—a lot of people don't know there was a sloth at the manger, but it doesn't say there wasn't. At St. Clement's, we also had a cat at the manger: it was a barn, for goodness' sake. There must have been a cat.

I am no longer as tired and ill as I was in my last days there. I have energy now. I no longer long to be slow and motionless. I'm back at the gym. At the gym, I wear a sloth t-shirt Patti O'Kane gave me. The sloth smiles on my chest as I pedal and step, lift and push—he is all that remains of my old exhaustion. It's so good to feel strong again.

But I still love the sloths. I love their determined boycott of the race of life—sloths ain't goin' nowhere. I love their improbable survival within a set of parameters that would seem certain to ensure their extinction—an animal that can't run? How is it that you're still here? But they *are* still here. Still slow. Still sloths. Ahh.

The Woodpecker Lollipop

Yesterday I made a woodpecker lollipop. Here is how: I took a 15-foot bamboo pole—the Geranium Farm is infested with bamboo—and coated the top ten inches or so with peanut butter. Then I stuck woodpecker food into the peanut butter, and tied the pole to the tree outside my office window where I can see it. When the woodpeckers have polished off the peanut butter and the seeds, I can untie the pole and reload.

Q was skeptical. *That's too green,* he said, *it'll break.*

Not under the weight of a woodpecker, I replied, sure of myself.

Under the weight of a squirrel it will.

Oh. Damn. I had forgotten about the squirrels. Well, we shall see. Actually, the flexibility of the green bamboo presents an interesting possibility: it might function as a kind of catapult for the squirrels if they get on the end of the pole, sending them flying across the yard. A sight I'd like to see, if only once.

The downy woodpecker in my tree needs a lollipop because the purple finches won't let him come near the feeder. Only Woody the Woodpecker is brash and self-confident—real woodpeckers are a little timid. Ours creeps down the tree trunk upside down, gazes longingly at the hanging feeder, reluctant to make the leap toward it, while all around him noisy finches flutter and chirp and fight about who's going to get which perch. The lollipop is just for him—he doesn't need a perch, and his kind is said to adore peanut butter. I like it, too. I helped myself to some of his while I was making his lollipop.

The lollipop seems to me like an idea that will work. I enjoyed thinking it up. It has all the right things about it: it's fast, cheap, simple. If it doesn't work, there's no great harm done.

Some things should be exhaustively planned ahead and researched. Some things can just be grabbed and tried. Sometimes there's such a thing as too much information—you can spend so much time making absolutely sure something will work that you never get around to actually doing it.

The Silence of the Bees

The Echinacea in our front garden attracts great insects. Little white common butterflies are always there. The other day I saw a gorgeous big monarch, and I have seen several other lovely stained-glass-looking butterflies whose names I don't know. Bees, most of all: lovely fat bumblebees. It is common to see two dozen bees on the pink/purple cone-shaped centers of the blooms of the six or seven plants that stand tall together in the garden, their furry striped bee bodies busily burrowing into the centers of the flowers, hovering in the air above a bloom to select the next target, sucking intently at the nectar, their thoraxes gently pulsing with the effort. I am not scared of the bees—it is safe to touch them. They are way too busy to bother with me.

Yesterday I had a scare. Up before the sun had really gotten going, I went out to admire the garden. In the cool of the morning, all the plants stood tall and strong and beautiful. I saw a bee on an Echinacea petal. He was curiously still. I went closer to look. No movement. I touched him gently with the tip of my finger—a leg moved slightly, but he did not recoil from my touch, as one might expect. And there, on another blossom, were two bees, one on top of the other, also still, also unresponsive. And on the underside of the petals of several blooms, more bees: still, betraying ongoing life only by the slightest wave of a leg, pulse of a thorax. They were all silent. Not a one was flying. None of them were moving at all.

Oh, no.

What was wrong with them? I went to find Q. Together we peered at the motionless bees. We didn't put anything *on* those plants, did we? I asked. No, he said, and continued to peer at the bees.

An hour later, I came around the side of the house and there they all were, busy as usual, going about their bee tasks with the single-mindedness that always makes me smile. They're all right. I now think that they don't get moving until the sun actually hits them. They're sort of like people who are just no good until they've had their coffee.

I had been heartbroken: where had I failed in the hospitality I was offering to the bees? Had I poisoned them? Was the agreeable buzz of activity I loved to watch about to become the stillness of death? One of the loveliest things about working with plants is that they attract animals, so many different kinds of animals. You have the opportunity to offer a welcome to creatures whose dignity does not derive from you. The animals that visit the garden are wild. They don't define themselves by our actions. They are about their own business. All we get is the chance to see them do it, and make their lives sweeter for a moment by offering them a treat along the road of their independent lives.

If the wild animals of the garden were to disappear, the effect on us would be more than just a honey shortage. The plants would soon follow: they depend on these tiny animals to continue their lives, spreading their pollen around the world so that new plants will appear. Everything is connected in the natural world, and seeing it reminds us that everything is connected in the whole of the domain of God, in which everything that is and that has been and that will ever be, lives. Whether we are close or have never met, it is still true that I would not be me if you were not you. We keep each other alive and well. Just by living together.

Heaven

Nine and a half hours—each way—with two teenagers in a Volkswagen Jetta. It should have been hell, but it wasn't. Rosie and Madeline were saints, just about. We stayed at the same Holiday Inn in Pennsylvania on the way back that we patronized on the way out to Ohio—tradition is so important for young people. On the way out, we shared the hotel with the Dubois High School Class of 1982. On the way back, it was the '62s—grayer hair, toddler grandchildren instead of teenaged children.

The waitress at breakfast was wearing a handmade red-white-and-blue ribbon, braided in a special way I had not seen before.

"That's really nice," I said, reaching out and touching it.

"My girlfriend made a bunch of them," she said.

"It's beautifully made."

"I try to wear it most days," she said, and nodded slightly.

"Hard to believe it's going to be a year soon, huh?" I said. Our eyes met, and suddenly it was as if we were somewhere else: in a funeral parlor, maybe, or in a church somewhere, or in a hospital waiting room. Not a Holiday Inn breakfast room. Suddenly it was as if a mutual friend had died, someone close, and we were meeting for the first time since the service. But I had never seen her before. We were strangers.

Earlier in the week, someone out in Ohio had asked me about the rebuilding at the World Trade Center site, and I surprised myself by the sudden awareness of tears in my eyes when I talked about the footprints of the buildings. About how I thought it ought to be a beautiful park. A place where people can go and see green, walk in beauty, feel the breeze from the river. Maybe with the names of those who died engraved somewhere—on a wall? On pavement stones? On wind chimes that would sing when the wind came? Something beautiful. Something healing. I realized, for the first time, that I feel strongly about it: I don't want to see that spot covered over with office buildings.

I guess I still can't believe they're gone. It still feels utterly new and foreign to me. It's still incomprehensible, still a shock, still an open wound, still an outrage, although I do not feel outraged. I'm still too weak to be outraged. I'm still just heartbroken.

A year after a death is a special time, a special, strange, passive re-injury. *Okay, I've gone a year,* you think—*let's get back to normal now. Give me my lost one back now, now that I've proven I can go without him, like a good, strong girl. I did my part. I was brave. So give him back.*

But we don't get them back. We don't get them back if we're not brave, and we don't get them back if we are. We just don't get them back.

"I still don't believe it."

"Me, neither," was all she said, and shook her head sadly. She went back to her trays. The girls were already headed back to the room, and it was time to get on the road. The waitress and I would never see each other again. But we had helped each other a little, showing each other our wounds like that. Our surprise at how much they still bled.

I believe in heaven. I believe the dead are there immediately—wherever and whatever "there" is, I know it is good. I trust in this completely. I have put my whole life on the line for it.

We believe. But that doesn't mean we don't still bleed.

Heaven must taste like Jersey tomatoes, Genevra emailed. We had brought her a bunch as a bribe, to convince her to let us spend the night on our way to Stratford for the Shakespeare Festival. It worked: not only did we get a bed for the night, we got a dinner party that really *was* like heaven: a dozen or so good people, each armed with a dish to share, sitting on a patio among the potted plants, a dinner party so sweet that it still seemed like fun to the two diners who got stung by bees. Yup, that's probably what heaven is like: everybody brings something, the bee stings don't matter much, people who don't know each other well—or at all—are instant friends. When Jesus compared the Kingdom of God to a banquet, he probably meant a potluck.

On our way back from Stratford, we inflicted ourselves on the Calverts. George is Q's college chum, and he and Buffy now live in tiny Andes, New York, after decades of ministry in a wondrous church in East Harlem. We arrived just in time to accompany them to the annual picnic meeting of the Andes Forum, a society formed to provide a place for young people to socialize. Most of the young people are now in their seventies. The meeting was brief but pithy: the club made some money on the recent strawberry festival, some of which will go to a mission in Ethiopia and some of which will go to buy a trombone for a young woman in town who's setting off for college—she's been using the school trombone up until now—and some of which will be saved for the next strawberry festival, I guess.

Heaven is probably like that, too: old friends to whom the passing years have been alternately gentle and cruel, changed and also *not* changed by life and the passage of time. In heaven, the sweet sameness of daily life is not marred by the pain that always accompanies it here. Those moments—rare in our experience—when we look around and say to ourselves *Oh, how lovely and how precious all this is* are all the time.

Back in New York. Hot, hot. Loud. Searching the sidewalk for alleys of shade in which to walk. Ozone alert: senior citizens in cooling centers. And back to the quiet convent room in which spiritual direction pursues its gardener-like cultivation of the soul: nourishment and cool water to the roots, air and space to breathe, encouraging the tropism all human beings have—we are all reaching for the sun. All of us.

Oh, how lovely and how precious.

I swear I didn't even move—I was just lying here asleep, minding my own business. Why would my knee begin to hurt? For no reason? The pain wakes me up, and soon I am awash in self-pity.

This is the thing about arthritis that I didn't realize until I had it: it's not just *activity* that makes it worse. It's also *inactivity*. Now what's that about? One or the other, please. But most patients have an especially bad time at night, and most patients are regularly awakened by pain. Makes no sense, but there it is.

You can get up and move around a bit, and it usually helps. Sometimes I pull the covers off the offending leg and lift it skyward, bending repeatedly at the knee, twenty or thirty times in the dark, hearing the scary crunch of bone, feeling the strange splinted stiffness in a joint that used to be so flexible. It would scare a burglar out of our room, if there ever were one: one long leg, rising with no warning from the silent bed, bending, flexing, bending, flexing, silently. He'd be back out the window in no time.

I sleep again. An old woman in my dream asks me to show her my legs. I think she may be God, but she is also a dance teacher. *What happened to your legs?* she asks, *show me.*

And I show her, like a child displays a skinned knee. *This one is from when the car hit me,* I say, showing her the faint scar from the contusion and the network of spidery blue veins below it, the swollen place in the ankle that never goes away, *and this one is the arthritis,* I say, showing her the swollen knee. *I didn't hurt the knee, I tell her, just the hip above it. And it was ten years ago. But now the knee is bad on that side.*

She holds each leg in her hands and examines each one closely and kindly. *I know,* she says.

I was a dancer, I say. At the gym earlier in the day, I couldn't achieve my usual wide stretch on the abductor machine. *I was a dancer,* I said to the machine. The machine didn't say anything.

I know you were, the old woman says, and strokes my knee once or twice. Kind.

She loves the misshapen ankle, the old scar, the painful joint.

Somehow, I know that this is not just a dream about me. It is also about us. Our city is like this, too. Bruised, even now, a year later. Bruised forever. Misshapen, disoriented. Moving along, to be sure, but always with a limp. You raise your eyes when you come out of the subway in Lower Manhattan to see where you are, and those large presences are not there to tell you. You approach by train, and that sterile gap in the skyline makes it shapeless, makes it no different from any other skyline anywhere, makes your heart sink. *For your servants love her very rubble,* says Psalm 102, appointed for this morning, *and are moved to pity even for her dust.*

I used to be a dancer, it says to me as I look out the train window across the Hudson River. I touch the window with my finger, tracing on the skyline the place where the World Trade Center would be. *I know.*